D0252620

AROUND THE WORLD WITH
80
WORDS

AROUND THE WORLD WITH
80
WORDS

Charles Berlitz

CASTLE BOOK**S**

This edition published in 2005 by
CASTLE BOOKS ®
A division of Book Sales, Inc.
114 Northfield Avenue
Edison, NJ 08837

This edition published by arrangement with
Charles Berlitz

Copyright © 1991 by Charles Berlitz. All rights reserved.

All rights reserved. No part of this book may be reproduced, stored in a
retrieval system, or transmitted in any form or by any means electronic
or mechanical including photocopying, recording or otherwise without
the prior permission in writing from the copyright owner and Castle Books.

Library of Congress Cataloging-in-Publication Data:

Berlitz, Charles, date.
Around the world with 80 words / Charles Berlitz.
p.   cm.
English language—Conversation and phrasebooks—Polyglot.
I.   Title. II. Title: Around the world with eighty words.

PE1131.B39   1991   89-24323 CIP
418—dc20

ISBN-13: 978-0-7858-1826-7
ISBN-10: 0-7858-1826-X

Printed in the United States of America

Acknowledgments

The author wishes to express his appreciation to the linguistic experts whose names are listed below, who have contributed valuable suggestions, expertise, calligraphy, and examination of the material in this book and the basic theory behind it.

Ahmet Ali Anslan, Turkish

Deolinda Avelar, Portuguese

Lin Berlitz, Researcher

Valerie Berlitz, Editor

Carmen Bowen, Swedish

Rita Browe, Danish

Johana Hal-na Chu, Chinese

Zofia Czernowsky, Polish

Astrid de Grabowski, Polish

Frank Hartman, Korean

The Imam Nipham Hasaan, Arabic

Kwi Sun Park, Korean

Rabbi R. A. Leiberman, Hebrew

Anna Mayol, Swedish

Anna Mertvago, Hungarian

Khanya Mool-siri, Thai

Somsri Pankam, Thai

Hemerit Parikh, Hindi

Kathryn Sears, Chinese

Mayumi Ogasawara Simms, Japanese

Dr. Alexander Song, Korean

Darayus Toot, Hindi

Hendrik Vietor, Dutch, Italian

Giselle Vorst, Hungarian

Elfrida Wierda, Dutch

Wu Yu-Chün-Wü, Chinese

Lisa Wager, Editor for Publisher

Edward Olinger, Assistant Editor

And especially to the following multilinguists who can express their linguistic opinions in a great variety of languages, ancient and modern:

Dr. George Frangos, university professor of social history and history of languages;

Charles Hughes, philologist, author, specialist in European, African, and Amerindian languages;

Dr. Constantine Mertvago, United Nations simultaneous interpreter of Russian, Greek, German, French, Italian.

And finally, or primarily, to his grandfather, Maximilian Delphinius Berlitz, linguist extraordinary, who established his language schools throughout the world more than one hundred years ago.

Some years ago a young Australian, Valerie Seary, took a course in Spanish at the Berlitz School of Languages in Sydney. Since that linguistic beginning she has become a researcher and multilingual editor of many books in many languages.

Around the World with 80 Words is dedicated—with appreciation and admiration to her—Valerie Seary Berlitz.

Contents

Introduction

Mark Twain once said that all he needed to enjoy the Germany of his day were three German words, those for "beer," "kiss," and "Thank you"—but international travel and communication have changed quite a bit since then. English-speaking travelers now visit every corner of the globe, and their needs are likely to be a little more complicated than those Twain described. Yet even today a traveler in a foreign country can make basic contact and express his needs with a surprisingly small vocabulary—one small enough to commit to memory.

At home, in our now cosmopolitan world, being able to speak in a foreign language is a definite aid to international and public relations—and abroad it is often a necessity. The world may be getting geographically smaller, but emotionally and linguistically it is growing, as the non-European languages of Asia and Africa take an increasingly important role in politics and business.

English is now considered to be the international language of business and air travel, but it is still advisable and often necessary, when you are traveling, to be able to use key words of communication in the world's most important languages and to have these key words at your fingertips wherever you are. Remember that less than 10 percent of the world's population speaks English.

Around the World with 80 Words contains a selective vocabulary adapted to each of twenty-five principal travel and business languages. You can absorb each mini–language course quickly and without prior preparation. Simply memorize the relatively brief list of words and a few numbers. The eighty words (some are phrases or brief sentences, actually) themselves are generally short and easy to remember. You may be able to learn them all in the time it takes you to fly to your destination.

Consider the eighty words as a tool for getting along abroad. They are a special passport for breaking the language barrier, for making friends, and an important step in the appreciation of foreign cultures. At first you may use your new vocabulary haltingly, but soon you will grow enthusiastic as you observe the pleased reactions of the people you are addressing. You may even get some extra mileage out of your new multilingual abilities by using them with the many foreign nationals traveling through the English-speaking world.

When the world was younger by several millennia, there were 10,000 spoken languages on the planet. The twenty-five languages dealt with in this book are only a handful of the 2,796 languages still spoken in the world (according to the Académie Française), but I have chosen them as the most important ones for travelers. More than half of them are the world's truly international languages today. *Around the World with 80 Words* presumes not to *teach* twenty-five languages but to give you a usable base, a foundation that will increase your enjoyment of foreign countries and their people.

I hope this successful start will inspire you to go further in your language studies and incline you toward the wisdom of a metaphor proposed to me at an early age by my grandfather M. D. Berlitz. He said, "Speaking only one language is like living in a great mansion of many rooms, each filled with fascinating treasures, but staying always in one room only. To visit the other rooms we need keys. These keys are the languages of the world we live in."

HOW TO USE
AROUND THE WORLD WITH 80 WORDS

The initial vocabulary section for each language has three columns. The left column shows the words in English. The middle column shows how they are written in the foreign language. The right column shows how to pronounce the words. The pronunciation column is written in short syllables which should be spoken as if you were reading them in English. Syllables written in capital letters should be stressed. A brief pronunciation guide at the beginning of each chapter or later in the chapter explains how to pronounce certain letters or letter combinations, or special accents or marks indicated in the middle and right columns. (Written accents in the *middle* column are expressed in the column at the right.)

When asking questions or making a request to a

stranger in a foreign country, remember to use the expression for "Mr.," "Mrs.," or "Miss," and to preface your remarks with "Please" or "Excuse me." All these words have advantages beyond politeness, since by using them you automatically put the person you are addressing in a good mood and prepare that person for your question. And always say "Thank you," perhaps the friendliest words in any language.

At the end of each vocabulary section you'll find the way to say "What is this?"—a very useful means of building your own vocabulary. When you're with local people, try pointing to things around you and asking what they're called in the native language. ("Credit card" usually needs no translation.) Remember that when you say a word aloud in a new language, you have a much better chance of remembering it than by simply reading the word or hearing it spoken.

NUMBERS

Numbers, of course, are important not only for prices and paying but also in addresses; telephone, floor, and room numbers; passport and car registration numbers; and driver's licenses. The "Arabic" numerals we use came to Europe as a result of the Crusades, but they are modified somewhat from the original Arabic numerals. However, we still follow the same decimal system developed by ancient Arab mathematicians.

If you write a number, chances are excellent that almost every foreigner will understand it. But for speaking purposes you should memorize how to say the numbers from 0 to 20 and to 100 by tens. The foreign words for other numbers, including 100, 100,000, and beyond (to be used according to your financial position, your tastes, or the currency in which you are dealing) are also listed.

FOREIGN WORDS YOU ALREADY KNOW

In almost every language there is a shortcut to increasing your vocabulary by recognizing which words are almost the same, in meaning and in spelling, as their English counterparts. There are thousands of these words in the Western European languages. With the key to each word you open your vocabulary to a great variety of foreign words—words that sound foreign only because they are pronounced differently.

SOME COMMON EXPRESSIONS

Each language chapter features a short list of words you will hear frequently in a given country. People seem to use them in almost every conversation. These are not included in the eighty-word list, but since they are so common in each language it is to your advantage to know what they mean. Try to become familiar with them.

INTERNATIONAL WORDS

Because of the activities and travel habits of people in the English-speaking nations, as well as the influence of television, movies, sports, and finance, many English words are now understood and used in all parts of the world. ("Okay" is a good example.) At the end of this book is a list of words that are products of various languages. These words are used and understood throughout the world. This list increases every year and may eventually form the basis of a truly international language for our planet. But until we have that, there is no substitute for the pleasure you experience from a language breakthrough, nor for the respect you express by speaking to someone in his or her own language.

French

French	Français	frahn-say

NOTE: In the right column, "n" represents a nasal "n" said through the nose; ů is pronounced by saying "ee" with the lips held in a tight circle; and zh is pronounced like the s in "pleasure." There is a slight stress on the last syllable of all the words.

Good day	Bonjour	bohn-ZHOOR
Good evening	Bon soir	bohn SWAR
How are you?	Comment allez-vous?	kohm-mawn tahl-lay-VOUS
Very well	Très bien	tray B'YEN
Happy to meet you	Enchanté	ahn-shawn-TAY
Good-bye	Au revoir	o ruh-VWAHR
My name	Mon nom	mohn nohn
Your name	Votre nom	votr' nohn
Mr. (and) Mrs.	Monsieur (et) Madame	muh-s'YERR (eh) ma-DAHM

Miss	Mademoiselle	mahd-mwa-ZELL
Yes	Oui	wee
No; not	Non; pas	nohn; pa
Excuse me	Pardon	par-DOHN
Please	S'il vous plaît	seel-voo-PLAY
Thank you	Merci	mehr-SEE
You're welcome	De rien	duh r'YEN
Again	Encore	ahn-KOR
Wait	Attendez	ah-tahn-DAY
Enough	Assez	ah-SAY
Where is	Où est	oo ay
the telephone	le téléphone	luh teh-leh-FOHN
the toilet	la toilette	la twa-LETT
the airport	l'aéroport	la-ah-eh-ro-POR
the train station	la gare	la gar
the subway	le métro	luh meh-TRO

my baggage	mes bagages	may ba-GAHZH
the train for ___	le train pour ___	luh trehn poor ___
the bus for ___	l'autobus pour ___	lo-toh-BŬS poor ___
the boat for ___	le bateau pour ___	luh ba-TOH poor ___
What time?	Quelle heure?	kel err
Now; not now	Maintenant; pas maintenant	mahnt-NAHN; pa mahnt-nahn
Later	Plus tard	plŭ tar
A bank	Une banque	ŭne bahnk
A drugstore	Une pharmacie	ŭne far-ma-SEE
A taxi	Un taxi	uhn tahk-SEE
A market	Un marché	uhn mar-SHAY
A department store	Un grand magasin	uhn grahn ma-ga-ZEN
Far; not far	Loin; pas loin	l'wahn; pa l'wahn
Left; right	Gauche; droit	gohsh; dr'wa
Here; there	Ici; là	ee-see; la

Open; closed	Ouvert; fermé	oo-VAIR; fair-MAY
Beautiful	Beau (m); belle (f)	bo; bell
How much?	Combien?	kohm-B'YEN
Very expensive	Très cher	tray shair
Less expensive	Moins cher	mwen shair
Another color	Une autre couleur	ůne otr' koo-LERR
Larger	Plus grand	plů grahn
Smaller	Plus petit	plů puh-TEE
The hotel	L'hôtel	lo-TEL
A room (with bath)	Une chambre (avec bain)	ůne shawmbr' (ah-VEK ban)
Today	Aujourd'hui	o-zhoor-DWEE
Tomorrow	Demain	duh-MEN
____ days*	____ jours	____ zhoor
What number?	Quel numéro?	kell nů-meh-RO
Good; not good	Bon; pas bon	bohn; pa bohn

*For numbers see page 22.

A restaurant	Un restaurant	uhn ress-ta-RAHN
Soup	De la soupe	duh la soop
Meat	De la viande	duh la v'yawnd
Chicken	Du poulet	du poo-LAY
Fish	Du poisson	du pwa-SOHN
An omelet	Une omelette	ůne om-LETT
Vegetables	Des légumes	deh leh-GŮME
Potatoes	Des pommes	deh pom
Bread	Du pain	dů pan
Mineral water	De l'eau minérale	duh lo mee-neh-RAL
Wine (or) beer	Du vin (ou) de la bière	dů van (oo) duh la b'yair
Coffee; tea	Du café; du thé	dů ka-FEH; dů tay
Milk	Du lait	dů lay
Dessert	Du dessert	dů dess-AIR
Delicious	Délicieux	day-lee-S'YUH
Police	Police	po-LEESS

Doctor	Médecin	med-SEN
Dentist	Dentiste	dahn-TEEST
Sick	Malade	ma-LAHD
Pain	Douleur	doo-LERR
Do you understand?	Comprenez?	kohm-pruh-NAY
I don't understand	Je ne comprends pas	zhuh nuh kohm-prawn PA
Slowly	Doucement	doos-MAHN
Possible	Possible	po-SEEBL'
What is this?	Qu'est-ce que c'est?	kess-kuh SAY

NUMBERS

0	zéro	zeh-ro
1	un(m); une(f)	un; ûne
2	deux	duh
3	trois	trwa
4	quatre	katr'
5	cinq	sank
6	six	sees

7	sept	set
8	huit	weet
9	neuf	nuhf
10	dix	deess
11	onze	ohnz
12	douze	dooz
13	treize	trez
14	quatorze	ka-TORZ
15	quinze	kenz
16	seize	sez
17	dix-sept	dees-SET
18	dix-huit	deez-WEET
19	dix-neuf	deez-NUHF
20	vingt	ven
21	vingt-et-un*	vent-ay-UN
30	trente	trahnt
40	quarante	karant
50	cinquante	sen-KAHNT
60	soixante	swa-SAHNT

*Words for numbers such as 21 that end in 1 have *et* (and) before the *un* (one); words for 22, 23, 32, and so on have no *et*. Thus, *vingt-et-un, trente-et-un,* and so on, but *vingt-deux, vingt-trois, trente-quatre.*

70	soixante-dix	swa-sahnt-DEESS
80	quatre-vingts	katr'-VEN
90	quatre-vingt-dix	katr'-ven-DEES
100	cent	sahn
1,000	mille	meel
100,000	cent mille	sahn-meel
1,000,000	un million	un meel-YOHN

In a unique linguistic survival, the words for 80 and 90 are based on the word for 20 *(vingt)*. This probably dates back to the time of ancient Gaul, and to the practice of counting on ten fingers *and* ten toes.

For Telling Time

Heure ("hour") is feminine and that is why an *e* is added to *un* to say "one o'clock." The other numbers do not change for gender.

What time is it?	Quelle heure est-il?	kell err eh-teel
One o'clock	Une heure	ûne err
Ten past one	Une heure dix	ûne err deess

Half past one	Une heure et demie	ûne err eh duh-mee
Five to two (two less five)	Deux heures moins cinq	duhz zerr mwoin sank
At three o'clock	À trois heures	ah trwa zerr

FRENCH

When William I, the French Duke of Normandy, conquered England in 1066, English went into a decline, becoming the language of serfs. French became the language of government and culture, and remained so until English-speaking kings took over parts of France and English resurfaced. As a result, the French language contains thousands of words that are almost the same in English but are generally unrecognizable when spoken rapidly in French. When a change of accent and/or spelling is recognized and approximated, English-speakers can use these thousands of shared words.

Most polysyllabic words in English are of French Norman origin—those dealing with literature, art, theater, medicine, and luxurious living, and a host of other words not connected with the work of the Anglo-Saxon serfs who tilled the fields and tended the livestock for the French-speaking overlords. Only in English do we have different words for edible farm animals—one word for the animal when alive and another to describe the animal when it is served as meat at the table. The Saxon word *steer* on the range; *beef* (from the French word *boeuf*) on the table. *Pig* in the sty; *pork* (*porc*) on the plate; and so on. More than forty percent of modern English comes from words of French Norman origin and, before that, Latin and to a lesser extent Greek.

Consider the following:

1. Many English words ending with *-tion* have the same spelling and meaning in French and English: *révolution, attention.*

2. The same is true of many words ending in *-able* or *-ible,* such as *possible, probable.*

3. This applies also to words ending in *-age,* such as *courage, garage, massage.*

4. And it is true of nouns ending in *-ent,* such as *president.*

5. French words ending in *-té* correspond to English words with a *-ty* ending: *qualité/quality.*

6. French words ending in *-thie* correspond to English words ending in *-thy: sympathie/sympathy.*

7. Hundreds of French social, artistic, and literary expressions used in English keep their French pronunciation: *bon voyage, cabaret, salon, école,* and so on.

With so many words in common one would think that English- and French-speakers would automatically understand each other, yet this is not the case. But once you overcome the pronunciation obstacle and say -tion as "s'yohn"; courage as "koo-rahzh"; possible as "po-seebl'," you will have added well over a thousand words to your French vocabulary.

FRENCH WORDS YOU ALREADY KNOW

A number of English words have invaded French in recent years: *star, weekend, best-seller, five-o'-clock tea, self-service, boyfriend, sandwich, gangster, gentleman,* and *businessman* are only a few.

SOME COMMON EXPRESSIONS

Voilà	vwa-la	That's it; Here it is
Bonne chance	bonn shawnss	Good luck
À votre santé!	ah vo-truh sahn-tay	To your health!
Bon appétit	bohn ah-pay-tee	Enjoy your meal
Vous désirez?	voo day-zee-ray	You wish something?
Comment?	ko-men	What? How?
C'est tout?	say too	Is that all?

Vraiment?	vray-mahn	Really?
N'est-ce pas?	ness-pa	Isn't it so?
Je vous en prie	zhuh voo sahn pree	Please go ahead; You first; You are too kind
Suivez-moi	swee-vay mwa	Follow me

Some words of endearment:

Chéri (m); chérie (f)	shay-ree	Dear (one)
Mon amour	mohn ah-moor	My love

And otherwise:

Imbécile	am-bay-seel	Imbecile
Crétin	cray-ten	Idiot
Allez-vous-en!	ah-lay voo-sahn	Get lost! Go away!

Spanish

Spanish	Español	ess-pahn-YOHL

NOTE: The double *l* (*ll*) in Spanish is pronounced almost like the *y* in "yellow"; *ñ* is pronounced like the *ny* in "canyon."

Good day	Buenos días	BWEH-nohs DEE-yahs
Good evening	Buenas noches	BWEH-nahs NO-chehs
How are you?	¿Cómo está usted?	KO-mo ess-TA oo-STED
Very well	Muy bien	mwee b'YEN
Happy to meet you	Mucho gusto	MOO-cho GOO-sto
Good-bye	Adiós	ah-d'YOHSS
My name	Mi nombre	mee NOHM-breh
Your name	Su nombre	soo NOHM-breh

Mr. (and)	Señor (y)	sen-YOHR
Mrs.	Señora	(ee) sen-YO-ra
Miss	Señorita	sen-yo-REE-ta
Yes	Sí	see
No; not	No	no
Excuse me	Perdón	per-DOHN
Please	Por favor	por fa-VOR
Thank you	Gracias	GRA-s'yahs
You're welcome	De nada	deh NA-da
Again	Otra vez	O-tra vess
Wait	Espere	ess-PEH-reh
Enough	Bastante	BA-stahn-teh
Where is	Dónde está	DOHN-deh ess-TA
the telephone	el teléfono	el teh-LEH-fo-no
the toilet	el excusado	el ess-koo-SA-doh
the airport	el aeropuerto	el ah-EH-ro-p'WER-toh
the train station	la estación de trenes	la ess-ta-s'YOHN deh TREHN-nehs

the subway	el metro	el MEH-tro
my baggage	mi equipaje	mee eh-kee-PA-heh
the train for___	el tren para___	el trehn PA-ra___
the bus for___	el autobus para ___	el ow-toh-BOOS PA-ra ___
the boat for ___	el barco para ___	el BAR-ko PA-ra ___
What time?	¿Qué hora?	keh O-ra
Now; not now	Ahora; no ahora	ah-O-ra; no ah-O-ra
Later	Más tarde	mahss TAR-deh
A bank	Un banco	oon BAHN-ko
A drugstore	Una farmacia	OO-na far-MA-s'ya
A taxi	Un taxi	oon TAHK-see
A market	Un mercado	oon mehr-KA-doh
A department store	Un almacén	oon-ahl-ma-SEN

Far; not far	Lejos; no lejos	LEH-hohs; no LEH-hohs
Left; right	Izquierdo; derecho	ees-k'YEHR-doh; deh-REH-cho
Here; there	Aquí; allí	ah-KEE; ah-YEE
Open; closed	Abierto; cerrado	ahb-YEHR-toh; ser-RA-doh
Beautiful	Bello (m); bella (f)	BEHL-yo; BEHL-ya
How much?	¿Cuánto?	KWAHN-toh
Very expensive	Muy caro	m'wee KA-ro
Less expensive	Menos caro	MEH-nohs KA-ro
Another color	Otro color	O-tra ko-LOHR
Larger	Más grande	mahss GRAHN-deh
Smaller	Más pequeño	mahs peh-KEHN-yo
The hotel	El hotel	el o-TEL

A room (with bath)	Un cuarto (con baño)	oon-KWAR-toh (kohn BAHN-yo)
Today	Hoy	oy
Tomorrow	Mañana	man-YA-na
____ days*	____ días	____ DEE-yahs
What number?	¿Qúe número?	keh NOO-meh-ro
Good; not good	Bueno; no bueno	BWEH-no; no BWEH-no
A restaurant	Un restaurante	oon res-toh-RAHN-teh
Soup	Sopa	SO-pa
Meat	Carne	KAR-neh
Chicken	Pollo	PO-l'yo
Fish	Pescado	peh-SKA-doh
Omelet	Tortilla de huevos	tor-TEEL-ya deh WEH-vohs
Vegetables	Verduras	vair-DOO-rahs

*For numbers see page 35.

Potatoes; rice	Papas; arroz	PA-pahs; ahr-ROHS
Bread	Pan	pahn
Mineral water	Agua mineral	AH-gwa mee-neh-RAHL
Wine (or) beer	Vino (o) cerveza	VEE-no (oh) sair-VEH-sa
Coffee; tea	Cafe; té	ka-FEH; teh
Milk	Leche	LAY-cheh
Dessert	Postre	PO-streh
Delicious	Delicioso	deh-lee-s'YO-so
Police	Policía	po-lee-SEE-ya
Doctor	Médico	MEH-dee-ko
Dentist	Dentista	den-TEE-sta
Sick	Enfermo	en-FAIR-mo
Pain	Dolor	doh-LOR
Do you understand?	¿Comprende?	kohm-PREN-deh
I don't understand	No comprendo	no kohm-PREN-doh
Slowly	Despacio	deh-SPA-s'yo
Possible	Posible	po-SEE-bleh

| What is this? | ¿Qué es esto? | kay ess ESS-toh |

NUMBERS

0	zero	SEH-ro
1	uno (m); una (f)	OO-no; OO-na
2	dos	dohs
3	tres	trayss
4	cuatro	KWA-tro
5	cinco	SEEN-ko
6	seis	sayss
7	siete	s'YAY-tay
8	ocho	OH-cho
9	nueve	N'WAY-vay
10	diez	d'yess
11	once	OHN-say
12	doce	DOH-say
13	trece	TRAY-say
14	catorce	ka-TOR-say
15	quince	KEEN-say

16	diez y seis	d'yess ee SAYSS
17	diez y siete	d'yess ee S'YAY-tay
18	diez y ocho	d'yess ee OH-cho
19	diez y nueve	d'yess ee N'WAY-vay
20	veinte	VAIN-tay
21 (etc.)	veinte y uno	vain-tee-OO-no
30	treinta	TRAIN-ta
40	cuarenta	kwa-REN-ta
50	cincuenta	seen-KWEN-ta
60	sesenta	say-SEN-ta
70	setenta	say-TEN-ta
80	ochenta	oh-CHEN-ta
90	noventa	no-VEN-ta
100	cien *or* ciento	s'yen; S'YEN-toh
1,000	mil	meel
100,000	cien mil	s'yen meel
1,000,000	un milión	oon meel-YOHN

For Telling Time

For starting time and making appointments, use the word *las* (plural for "the") before the number word, except for "one o'clock," which is simply *la una*.

What time is it?	¿Qué hora es?	kay OH-ra ess
It's one o'clock	Es la una	ess la OO-na
It's two o'clock	Son las dos	sohn lahss dohs
It's half past three	Son las tres y media	sohn lahss trehs ee MEHD'ya
It's ten to four	Son las cuatro menos diez	sohn lahss KWA-tro MEH-nohs d'yess
At five o'clock	A las cinco	ah lahs SEEN-ko

SPANISH

The official language of Spain and of nineteen republics in the Western Hemisphere, and widely spoken in the Philippines and parts of Africa, as well as the United States (where there are now well over 25 million speakers), Spanish is truly a world language. It is also spoken in the Mediterranean islands and even in Turkey, where the descendants of Spanish Jews, exiled from Spain over five hundred years ago, have zealously maintained medieval Spanish as a spoken language, in a remarkable example of language loyalty.

The Spanish-speaking population of the United States has grown steadily in recent years, and Americans have become familiar with many Spanish words—especially those used in the Southwest, where Spanish antedates English by more than two hundred years.

SPANISH WORDS YOU ALREADY KNOW

You already know a lot of Spanish words—all you have to do is to modify the spelling and the pronunciation. Because Spanish, like French, is a language descended from Latin, it is possible to transform many English words into Spanish when you consider the following:

1. Many English words that end in *-tion* end in *-ción* in Spanish (generally pronounced *s'yohn* in Latin America and *th'yohn* in much of Spain): *revolución, constitución,* and so on.

2. Many English words that end in *-ty* end in *-dad* in Spanish: *oportunidad, felicidad.*

3. The English word ending *-able* is often the same in Spanish: *probable, aceptable.*

4. The English word ending -*ible* is often the same in Spanish: *posible, imposible.*

5. Many English words that end in -*age* end in -*aje* in Spanish: *garaje, masaje.*

6. Many English words that end in -*ent* end in -*ente* in Spanish: *presidente, eminente.*

7. Many English words that end in -*ly* end in -*mente* in Spanish: *rapidamente, probablemente.*

In addition, a number of words used in the American West and in cowboy movies have been adopted from Spanish, sometimes with different spellings or changes in meaning.

ENGLISH ADAPTATION	ORIGINAL SPANISH MEANING
bronco	rough, angry (not necessarily a horse)
mustang	strayed (*mesteño*)
lasso	knot (*lazo*)
lariat	rope, lasso (*reata*)
calaboose	cell, prison (*calabozo*)
desperado	desperate (*desesperado*)
loco	crazy
Colorado	colored; red

Montana	mountain (*montaña*)
Nevada	snowfall

SOME COMMON EXPRESSIONS

Hola*	OH-la	Hello
Dígame*	DEE-ga-meh	Tell me
¿Habla usted español?	AH-bla oo-STED ess-pahn-YOHL	Do you speak Spanish?
¡Salud!	sa-LOOD	To your health!
¡Que aproveche!	keh-ah-pro-VEH-cheh	May you enjoy it!
¡Olé!	oh-LAY	Well done! Bravo!
¿Qué quiere?	keh K'YEHR-reh	What do you want?
No sé	no seh	I don't know
¿Por qué no?	por keh no	Why not?
No importa	no eem-POR-ta	It doesn't matter
Buen viaje	bwen v'YA-heh	Have a good trip

*Often used when answering the phone.

Some words of endearment:

Querido (m)	keh-REE-doh	Loved one; dear
Querida (f)	keh-REE-da	Loved one; dear
Mi amor	mee ah-MOR	My love
Mi vida	mee VEE-da	My life

And otherwise:

Idiota	ee-D'YO-ta	Idiot
Bobo	BO-bo	Fool (m)
Boba	BO-ba	Fool (f)
Gringo*	green-go	American

*This term comes from an American song sung by U.S. troops during the Mexican War: "Where the *green* grass grows . . ." Definitely *not* a compliment.

German

German	Deutsch	doytch

NOTE: In German, *ä* is said as "eh," *ch* is "hk," *ö* is "er," and *ü* is pronounced by saying "ee" with the lips held in a tight circle. This is indicated by "u̇" in the third column. Nouns in German are always spelled with the first letter capitalized, whether they come at the beginning of a sentence or not.

Good day	Guten Tag	GOOT'en tahk
Good evening	Guten Abend	GOOT'en AH-bent
How are you?	Wie geht's?	vee gehts
Very well	Sehr gut	zair goot
Happy to meet you	Sehr erfreut	zair air-FROYT
Good-bye	Auf Wiedersehen	owf VEE-dair-zay'n
My name	Mein Name	mine NA-meh
Your name	Ihr Name	eer NA-meh

Mr. (and)	Herr (und)	hair (oont)
Mrs.	Frau	frow
Miss	Fräulein	FROY-line
Yes	Ja	ya
No; not	Nein; nicht	nine; nihkt
Excuse me	Verzeihung	fair-TS'EYE-oong
Please	Bitte	BIT-teh
Thank you	Danke schön	DAHN-keh shern
You're welcome	Bitte	BIT-teh
Again	Noch einmal	nohkh INE-mahl
Wait	Ein Moment	ine mo-MENT
Enough	Genug	geh-NOOK
Where is	Wo ist	vo isst
the telephone	das Telefon	dahss teh-leh-FOHN
the toilet	die Toilette	dee twa-LET-teh
the airport	der Flughafen	dair FLOOG-ha-fen

the train station	der Bahnhof	dair BAHN-hohf
the subway	die U-bahn	dee OO-bahn
my baggage	mein Gepäck	mine guh-PECK
the train for ____	der Zug nach ____	dair ts'oog nahkh ____
the bus for ____	der Bus nach ____	dair boos nahkh ____
the boat for ____	das Boot nach ____	dahss boat nahkh ____
What time?	Wie viel Uhr?	vee feel oor
Now; not now	Jetzt; nicht jetzt	yetst; nihkt yetst
Later	später	SHPAY-ter
A bank	Eine Bank	INE-eh bahnk
A drugstore	Eine Apotheke	INE-eh ah-po-TEH-keh
A taxi	Ein Taxi	ine tahk-see
A market	Ein Markt	ine markt
A department store	Ein Warenhaus	ine VA-ren-howss
Far; not far	Weit; nicht weit	vite; nihkt vite

Left; right	Links; rechts	links; rekhts
Here; there	Hier; dort	heer; dort
Open; closed	Offen; geschlossen	OFF-fen; geh-SHLO-sen
Beautiful	Schön	schern
How much?	Wie viel?	vee feel
Very expensive	Sehr teuer	zair TOY-er
Less expensive	Billiger	BIL-lig-er
Another color	Eine andere Farbe	INE-neh AHN-deh-reh FAR-beh
Larger	Grösser	GRER-ser
Smaller	Kleiner	KLY-ner
The hotel	Das Hotel	dahss oh-TEL
A room (with bath)	Ein Zimmer (mit Bad)	ine TSIM-mer (mitt bahd)
Today	Heute	HOY-teh
Tomorrow	Morgen	MOR-ghen
___ days*	___ Tage	___ TA-gheh
What number?	Welche Nummer?	VEL-kheh NOO-mer

*For numbers see page 47.

Good; not good	Gut; nicht gut	goot; nihkt goot
A restaurant	Ein Restaurant	ine ress-toh-RAHNT
Soup	Suppe	ZOOP-peh
Meat	Fleisch	flysh
Chicken	Huhn	hoon
Fish	Fisch	fish
Omelet	Omelett	ohm-LEHT
Vegetables	Gemüse	geh-MŮ-zeh
Potatoes	Kartofflen	kar-TOH-flen
Bread	Brot	broht
Mineral water	Mineralwasser	mee-neh-RAHL-va-ser
Wine (or) beer	Wein (oder) Bier	vine (OH-der) beer
Coffee; tea	Kaffee; Tee	kah-FAY; tay
Milk	Milch	meelkh
Dessert	Nachtisch	NAHKH-tish
Delicious	Köstlich	KERST-lick
Police	Polizei	po-lee-TZY
Doctor	Arzt	arts't
Dentist	Zahnarzt	TSAHN-arts't

Sick	Krank	krahnk
Pain	Schmerz	shmehrts
Do you understand?	Verstehen Sie?	Fair-SHTAY'en zee
I don't understand	Ich verstehe nicht	ikh fair-SHTAY-eh nihkt
Slowly	Langsam	LAHNG-sam
Possible	Möglich	MERG-likh
What is this?	Was ist das?	vahss isst dahss

NUMBERS

0	nul	nool
1	eins	ine'ss
2	zwei	ts'vy
3	drei	dry
4	vier	feer
5	fünf	fûnf
6	sechs	zeks
7	sieben	ZEE-ben
8	acht	ahkht

9	neun	noyn
10	zehn	ts'ayn
11	elf	elf
12	zwölf	ts'verlf
13	dreizehn	DRY-ts'ayn
14	vierzehn	FEER-ts'ayn
15	fünfzehn	FŮNF-ts'ayn
16	sechzehn	ZEKH-ts'ayn
17	siebzehn	ZEEP-ts'ayn
18	achtzehn	AHKH-ts'ayn
19	neunzehn	NOYN-ts'ayn
20	zwanzig	TS'VAHN-ts'ikh
21 (etc.)*	einundzwanzig	INE-oont-ts'vahn-ts'ikh (literally, "one and twenty")
30	dreißig	DRY-sikh
40	vierzig	FEER-ts'ikh
50	fünfzig	FŮNF-ts'ikh
60	sechzig	ZEKH-ts'ikh
70	siebzig	ZEEP-ts'ikh

*Note that 21, 22, and so on are expressed as "one and twenty," "two and twenty," and so forth.

80	achtzig	AHKH-ts'ikh
90	neunzig	NOYN-ts'ikh
100	(ein) hundert	(ine) HOON-dert
1,000	(ein) tausend	(ine) T'OW-zent
100,000	ein hundert-tausend	HOON-dert-t'ow-zent
1,000,000	eine million	INE-eh MIL-yohn

For Telling Time

"Half past" is expressed by saying halfway to the *next* hour.

What time is it?	Wieviel Uhr ist es?	vee feel oor isst ess
It's one o'clock	Es ist ein Uhr	ess isst ine oor
Two o'clock	Zwei Uhr	t'svy oor
Half past two (halfway to three)	Halb drei	hahlb dry
Ten minutes to three	Zehn Minuten vor drei	ts'ane mee-NOO-ten for dry

| At three o'clock | Um drei Uhr | oom dry oor |

GERMAN

German missed being the official language of the United States by one vote. When the thirteen American colonies broke away from England and were deciding what language they should officially adopt for the new country, the choice was among English, German (which at that time had the advantage of being spoken in many small European states as well as by the many German and Dutch people living in America), and curiously, Hebrew and ancient Greek—doubtlessly favored by churchmen and scholars. In the end English won by a single vote. But German scored a victory of sorts: the first newspaper report of the promulgation of the Declaration of Independence was printed in a German-language newspaper in Philadelphia.

As grammar and construction in English are much simpler than in German, the choice was easy for those who already spoke English. German vocabulary, however, is much simpler than it looks, principally because of the German tendency to link many words together as one, a constant source of wonder and amusement to students of German; consider, for instance, *Donaudampfschiffsfahrtsgesellschaftskapitän,* which means "captain of the Danube ship tour company."

GERMAN WORDS YOU ALREADY KNOW

As English-speakers considering German we find hundreds—even thousands—of words very close to our English ones. Most are of one or two syllables and all are everyday words easy to recognize by spelling or sound, such as the nouns *Haus, Maus, Katze, Land, Wagen, Papier, Bär* (bear), *Sommer, Ring, Wind,* and the adjectives *best, wild,* and *still* (quiet). (Note that nouns in German are written with an initial capital letter.) A number of German words have been adopted into English usage practically unchanged: *Kindergarten, Sauerkraut, Hamburger, Gesundheit, kaputt,* and *Blitzkrieg.* The German language has been augmented in recent years by such American imports as *babysitter, teenager, gangster, supermarket,* and *rock music.* (See also the list of international words on page 317).

Some German words sound exactly like English words but have quite different meanings. *Gift* in German means "poison," and *Mist* means "manure" or "trash." If it were not for the spelling and rather complicated grammar it would be easy for English-speakers to learn German quickly. It is in fact easier for German-speakers to learn English than vice versa; except for the pronunciation, Germans find English pleasantly simple, although to German eyes it seems somewhat inexact.

SOME COMMON EXPRESSIONS

Sprechen Sie deutsch?	SPREK-hen zee doytch	Do you speak German?
Sind Sie Amerikaner? (m)	zint zee ah-meh-ree-KA-ner	Are you American?
Sind Sie Amerikanerin? (f)	zint zee ah-meh-ree-KA-ner-in	Are you American?
Sind Sie Engländer? (m)	zint zee ENG-len-der	Are you English?
Sind Sie Engländerin? (f)	zint zee ENG-len-der-in	Are you English?
Was wünschen Sie?	vahss VÜN-shen zee	What do you wish? What would you like?
Was ist los?	vahss ist lohs	What's going on?
Warum nicht?	VA-room nikht	Why not?
Verboten	FAIR-bo-ten	Forbidden
Es macht nichts	ess mahkht nikhts	It doesn't matter

Einverstanden	INE-ver-shtahnd'en	Agreed
Mahlzeit	MAHL-ts'ite	Mealtime (said before eating, as "Enjoy your meal")
Prosit!	prohst	To your health!
Gute Reise	GOO-teh RY-zeh	Have a good trip
Kommen Sie bald wieder	Ko-men zee bahlt VEE-der	Come back soon

Some words of endearment:

Liebling	LEEB-ling	Little love; dear
Mein Schatz	mine shahtz	My treasure

And otherwise:

Dummkopf	DOOM-kohpf	Dumbhead
Schweinhund	SHVINE-hoondt	Pig-dog

Italian

Italian	Italiano	ee-tahl-YA-no
Good day	Buon giorno	bwohn JOR-no
Good evening	Buona sera	BWO-na SEH-ra
How are you?	Come sta?	KO-meh sta
Very well	Benissimo	beh-NEE-see-mo
Happy to meet you	Piacere	p'ya-CHEH-reh
Good-bye	Arrivederci	ah-ree-veh-DEHR-chee
My name	Mio nome	MEE-yo NO-meh
Your name	Suo nome	SOO-o NO-meh
Mr. (and) Mrs.	Signore (e) Signora	seen-YO-reh (eh) seen-YO-ra

Miss	Signorina	seen-yo-REE-na
Yes	Sì	see
No; not	No; non	no; nohn
Excuse me	Scusi	SCOO-zee
Please	Per piacere	pehr p'ya-CHEH-reh
Thank you	Grazie	GRA-ts'yeh
You're welcome	Prego	PREH-go
Again	Ancora	ahn-KO-ra
Wait	Aspetti	ah-SPEHT-tee
Enough	Basta	BA-sta
Where is	Dov'è	doh-VEH
the telephone	il telefono	eel teh-LEH-fo-no
the toilet	il gabinetto	eel ga-bee-NET-toh
the airport	l'aeroporto	la-eh-roh-POR-toh
the train station	la stazione di treni	la sta-T'SYO-neh dee TREH-nee

the subway	la metro-politana	la me-tro-po-lee-TA-na
my baggage	il mio bagaglio	eel MEE-yo ba-GA-l'yo
the train for ——	il treno per ——	eel TREH-no pehr ——
the bus for ——	l'autobus per ——	l'ow-toh-BOOSS pehr ——
the boat for ——	il battello per ——	eel baht-TEL-lo pehr ——
What time?	Che ora?	keh OH-ra
Now; not now	Adesso; non adesso	ah-DESS-so; nohn ah-DESS-so
Later	Più tardi	p'yoo TAR-dee
A bank	Una banca	OON-a BAHN-ka
A drugstore	Una farmacia	OO-na far-ma-CHEE-ya
A taxi	Un tassì	oon ta-SEE
A market	Un mercato	oon mehr-KA-toh

A department store	Un (grande) magazzino	oon (GRAHN-deh) ma-gaht-ZEE-no
Far; not far	Lontano; non lontano	lohn-TA-no; nohn lohn-TA-no
Left; right	Sinistro; destro	see-NEESS-tro; DEHSS-tro
Here; there	Qui; là	kwee; la
Open; closed	Aperto; chiuso	ah-PEHR-toh; K'YOO-zo
Beautiful	Bello (m) bella (f)	BEL-lo BEL-la
How much?	Quanto?	KWAHN-toh
Very expensive	Molto caro	MOHL-to KA-ro
Less expensive	Meno caro	MEH-no KA-ro
Another color	Un altro colore	oon AHL-tro ko-LO-reh
Larger	Più grande	pew GRAHN-deh

Smaller	Più piccolo	pew PEE-ko-lo
The hotel	L'albergo	lahl-BEHR-go
A room (with bath)	Una stanza (con bagno)	OO-na STAHN-tsa (kohn BAHN-yo)
Today	Oggi	Ohj-jee
Tomorrow	Domani	doh-MA-nee
____ days*	____ giorni	____ JOR-nee
What number?	Che numero?	keh NOO-meh-ro?
Good; not good	Buono; non buono	BWO-no; nohn BWO-no
A restaurant	Un ristorante	oon ree-sto-RAHN-teh
Soup	Minestra	mee-NEHSS-tra
Meat	Carne	KAR-neh
Chicken	Pollo	POHL-lo
Fish	Pesce	PEH-sheh
Omelet	Omelette	o-meh-LET-teh

*For numbers see page 60.

Vegetables	Legumi	lay-GOO-mee
Pasta	Pasta	PA-sta
Bread	Pane	PA-neh
Mineral water	acqua minerale	AH-kwa mee-neh-RA-leh
Wine (or) beer	vino (o) birra	VEE-no (o) BEER-ra
Coffee; tea	caffè; tè	kaf-FEH; teh
Milk	Latte	LAHT-teh
Dessert (sweet)	Dolce	DOHL-cheh
Delicious	Delizioso	deh-lee-T'ZYO-zo
Police	Polizia	po-lee-TS'EE-ya
Doctor	Dottore	doht-TOH-reh
Dentist	Dentista	dehn-TEE-sta
Sick	ammalato	AHM-ma-LA-toh
Pain	Dolore	doh-LO-reh
Do you understand?	Capisce?	ka-PEE-sheh
I don't understand	Non capisco	nohn ka-PEE-sko

Slowly	Piano	P'YA-no
Possible	Possibile	pos-SEE-bee-leh
What is this?	Cos'è?	ko-ZEH

NUMBERS

0	zero	tseh-ro
1	uno	OO-no
2	due	DOO-eh
3	tre	treh
4	quattro	KWAHT-tro
5	cinque	CHEEN-kweh
6	sei	say
7	sette	SEHT-teh
8	otto	OHT-toh
9	nove	NO-veh
10	dieci	D'YEH-chee
11	undici	OON-dee-chee
12	dodici	DOH-dee-chee
13	tredici	TREH-dee-chee

14	quattordici	kwaht-TOHR-dee-chee
15	quindici	KWEEN-dee-chee
16	sedici	SEH-dee-chee
17	diciassette	dee-chahss-SEHT-teh
18	diciotto	dee-CHOHT-toh
19	diciannove	dee-chah-NO-veh
20	venti	VEN-tee
21	ventuno*	ven-TOO-no
30	trenta	TREN-ta
40	quaranta	kwa-RAHN-ta
50	cinquanta	cheen-KWAHN-ta
60	sessanta	sess-SAHN-ta
70	settanta	seht-TAHN-ta
80	ottanta	oht-TAHN-ta
90	novanta	no-VAHN-ta

*Words for numbers such as 21 that end in 1 drop the final vowel in the "tens" element; otherwise they retain it: *ventuno* (21) but *ventidue, ventitre; quarantuno* (41) but *quarantadue, quarantatre;* and so on.

100	cento	CHEN-toh
1,000	mille	MEEL-leh
100,000	centomila	chen-toh-MEE-la
1,000,000	un milione	oon meel-YO-neh

For Telling Time

Use the plural article *le* (leh) before the number word—*le due, le tre,* and so on; for one o'clock, add only *l'*—*l'una* (LOO-nah). For the half-hour, add *e mezzo.*

What time is it?	Che ora è?	keh O-ra eh
It's two	Sono le due	SO-no leh DOO-weh
It's two-ten	Sono le due e dieci	SO-no leh DOO-weh eh D'YEH-chee
Half past two	Le due e mezzo	leh DOO-weh eh MED-d'zo
Ten to three	Le tre meno dieci	leh treh MEH-no D'YEH-chee
At three o'clock	Alle tre	AHL-leh treh

ITALIAN

Italian is spoken by more than 65 million people in Italy and the Italian islands of the Mediterranean, in southern Switzerland, parts of Tunis, Libya, and North Africa, and by millions more in the United States, Canada, Argentina, and Australia.

Italian is the closest linguistic descendant of Latin, the language of ancient Rome and the most important world language for over a thousand years. Until recently, Latin was the language of the Catholic Church, where it is still widely used. It also survives as a reference language of scholarship, medicine, and law.

Italian, French, Spanish, Catalán, Portuguese, Romansch (the fourth official language of Switzerland), and Romanian—the current languages of areas that were once part of the Roman Empire—are all descended from Latin, and known as the Romance languages. Modern Italian has deviated too much from the original Latin to be understood by a native Latin speaker, were there any left, but many of the Romance languages are mutually understandable to their indigenous speakers, especially Italian, Spanish, and Portuguese.

ITALIAN WORDS YOU ALREADY KNOW

Italian, being essentially a musical lanaguage, has contributed a great deal to the international vocabulary of music. The following examples are translated for everyday usage, which is sometimes different from the familiar musical connotation.

MUSICAL TERM	LITERAL MEANING(S) IN ITALIAN
adagio	slowly; softly
andante	going; current
basso	low
fortissimo	very strong; very loud
maestro	instructor; master; director
mezzo	middle
opera	work; action; performance
piano	slowly; flat; plan; floor (in a building)
presto	quickly; early; soon
profundo	deep (*profondo*)
tenore	contents; way

Because English has its roots in both Latin (dating from ancient and medieval times) and French (itself a Romance language), which was injected into developing English with the Norman conquest of England in 1066, almost half of English words are of Latin or Franco-Latin origin. Thus there are thousands of Italian words that are very easy to understand, since only a slight spelling difference and their pronunciation distinguishes them from their English counterparts.

fraternità	fraternity
libertà	liberty
società	society
possibile	possible
probabile	probable
naturalmente	naturally
normalmente	normally
rapidamente	rapidly
eccellente	excellent
evidente	evident
presidente	president
monumento	monument
supplemento	supplement

SOME COMMON EXPRESSIONS

Ciao	chow	Hi; Bye
Parla italiano?	PAR-la ee-tahl-YA-no	Do you speak Italian?

Mi dispiace	mee dis-P'YA-cheh	Excuse me; I'm sorry
Tante belle cose	TAHN-teh BEL-leh KO-zeh	Many beautiful things (a farewell greeting and a wish)
Ottimo	OHT-tee-mo	Great
Salute!	sa-LOO-teh	To your health! (also said after someone sneezes)
Perbacco!	pehr-BAK-ko	My goodness! (literally, "By Bacchus!": an ancient Roman interjection referring to Bacchus, god of wine)
Spero di sì	SPEH-ro dee see	I hope so
Vediamo	veh-D'YA-mo	Let's see
Buona fortuna	BWO-na for-TOO-na	Good luck

| A presto | ah PREH-sto | Till soon; See you soon |

Some terms of endearment:

Carissimo (m)	ka-REESS-see-mo	Beloved; dearest
Carissima (f)	ka-REESS-see-ma	Beloved; dearest
Amore mio	ah-MO-reh MEE-yo	My love
Ti voglio bene	tee VOHL-yo BEH-neh	I love you

And otherwise:

Va via!	va VEE-ya	Get lost!
Cretino	kreh-TEE-no	Stupid fool
Mascalzone	mahss-kahl-T'ZO-neh	Scoundrel

Portuguese

Portuguese	Português	por-too-GEHSS

NOTE: In Portuguese, a number of syllables ending in *-ais* are pronounced with a final "sh" sound; the letters *ão* are pronounced "oun," with the abbreviated nasal sound "n" at the end; *gh* and *j* are pronounced "zh"; the final *m* in a word is pronounced "n."

Good day	Bom dia	bohn DEE-ah
Good evening	Boa noite	BO-ah NOY-tee
How are you?	Como está?	KO-mo ehs-TA
Very well	Bem	behn
Happy (to meet you)	Muito prazer	MWEE-toh pra-ZEHR
Good-bye	Adeus	ah-DEH-ooss
My name	Meu nome	MEH-oo NO-meh
Your name	Seu nome	SEH-oo NO-meh

Mr. (and)	Senhor (e)	sehn-YOR
Mrs.	Senhora	(eh) sehn-YO-ra
Miss	Senhorita	sehn-yo-REE-ta
Yes	Sim	seen
No; not	não	noun
Excuse me	Desculpe-me	dehs-KOOL-peh-meh
Please	Por favor	por fa-VOR
Thank you	Obrigado (man speaker) Obrigada (woman speaker)	oh-bree-GA-doh oh-bree-GA-da
You're welcome	De nada	deh NA-da
Again	Outra vez	OOT-ra vez
Wait	Espere	ESS-peh-reh
Enough	Bastante	ba-TAHN-teh
Where is	Onde está	OHN-deh ehs-TA
the telephone	o telefone	oh teh-leh-FO-neh

the toilet	o toilette	oh twa-LEH-teh
the airport	o aeroporto	oh ah-eh-ro-POR-toh
the train station	a estação de trem	ah ehs-TA-sourr deh tren
the subway	o metro	oh MEH-tro
my baggage	a minha bagagem	ah meen-ya ba-GA-zhen
the train for ____	o trem para ____	oh tren PA-ra ____
the bus for ____	o ônibus para ____	oh OH-nee-boos PA-ra ____
the boat for ____	o barco para ____	oh BAR-ko PA-ra ____
What time?	Que horas?	keh OH-rahs
Now; not now	Agora; não agora	ah-GO-ra; nourr ah-GO-ra
Later	Mais tarde	maish TAR-deh
A bank	Um banco	oon BAHN-ko

A drugstore	Uma farmácia	OO-ma far-MA-s'ya
A taxi	Um táxi	oon TAHK-see
A market	Um mercado	oon mehr-KA-doh
A department store	Uma loja de departamentos	OO-ma LO-zha deh deh-par-ta-MEHN-tohss
Far; not far	Longe; não longe	LOHN-zheh; noun LOHN-zheh
Left; right	Esquerdo; direito	ehs-KEHR-doh; dee-RAY-toh
Here; there	Aqui, ali	ah-KEE; ah-LEE
Open; closed	Aberto; fechado	ah-BEHR-toh; feh-SHA-doh
Beautiful	Lindo (m) linda (f)	LEEN-doh LEEN-da
How much?	Quanto?	KWAHN-toh
Very expensive	Muito caro	MWEEN-toh KA-ro

Less expensive	Menos caro	MEH-nos KA-ro
Another color	Outra côr	OH-tra kohr
Larger	Mais grande	maysh GRAN-deh
Smaller	Mais pequeno	maysh peh-KEH-no
Hotel	Hotel	oh-TEHL
A room (with bath)	Um quarto (com banheiro)	oon KWAR-toh (kohn bahn-YEH-ro)
Today	Hoje	OH-zheh
Tomorrow	Amanhã	ah-mahn-YA
____ days*	____ dias	____ DEE-ahs
What number?	Que número?	keh NOO-meh-ro
Good; not good	Bom; não é bom	bohn; noun eh bohn
A restaurant	Um restaurante	oon rehs-ta-oo-RAHN-teh
Soup	Sopa	SO-pa
Meat	Carne	KAR-neh
Chicken	Galinha	ga-LEEN-ya

*For numbers see page 74.

Fish	Peixe	PAY-sheh
Omelet	Omelete	oh-meh-LET-teh
Vegetables	Legumes	leh-GOO-mehs
Rice	Arroz	ah-RROHSS
Bread	Pão	pouɴ
Mineral water	Água mineral	AH-gwa mee-neh-RAHL
Wine (or) beer	Vinho (o) cerveja	VEEN-yo (oh) sehr-VEH-zha
Coffee; tea	Café; chá	ka-FEH; sha
Milk	Leite	LAY-teh
Dessert	Sobremesa	so-breh-MEH-sa
Delicious	Delicioso	deh-lees-YO-so
Police	Polícia	po-LEES-ya
Doctor	Doutor	doh-TOHR
Dentist	Dentista	den-TEES-ta
Sick	Doente	doh-EHN-teh
Pain	Dôr	dohr
Do you understand?	Compreende?	kohm-preh-EN-deh

I don't understand	Não compreendo	noun kohm-preh-EN-doh
Slowly	Lentamente	len-ta-MEN-teh
Possible	Possível	po-SEE-vehl
What is this?	Que é isto?	keh eh EES-toh

NUMBERS

0	zero	ZEH-ro
1	um (m); uma (f)	oon; OO-ma
2	dois; (m); duas (f)	doys; DOO-ahs
3	três	trehs
4	quatro	KWA-tro
5	cinco	SEEN-ko
6	seis	says
7	sete	SEH-teh
8	oito	OY-toh
9	nove	NO-veh
10	dez	dehs
11	onze	OHN-zeh

12	doze	DOH-zeh
13	treze	TREH-zeh
14	quatorze	kwa-TOHR-zeh
15	quinze	KEEN-zeh
16	dezesseis	deh-zeh-SAYS
17	dezessete	deh-zeh-SEH-teh
18	dezoito	deh-ZOY-toh
19	dezenove	deh-zeh-NO-veh
20	vinte	VEEN-teh
21 (etc.)	vinte e um	VEEN-teh eh oon
30	trinta	TREEN-ta
40	quarenta	kwa-REHN-ta
50	cinqüenta	seen-KWEHN-ta
60	sessenta	seh-SEHN-ta
70	setenta	seh-TEHN-ta
80	oitenta	oy-TEHN-ta
90	noventa	no-VEHN-ta

100	cem; cento	sengh; SEHN-toh
1,000	mil	meel
100,000	cem mil	sengh meel
1,000,000	um milhão	oon meel-YOHNG

For Telling Time

"One" and "two" have masculine and feminine forms *(um, uma; dois, duas),* and *ora* is feminine. The numbers from three on are "unisex."

What time is it?	Que horas são?	keh OH-rahs soun
It's one o'clock	E uma hora	eh OO-na OH-ra
It's two o'clock	São duas horas	soun DOO-ahs OH-rahs
Ten past two	As duas eh dez	DOO-ahs OH-rahs eh dehs
Half past two	As duas meia	ahs DOO-ahs MEH-ya
Twenty to three	As três meno vinte	ahs trehs MEH-no VEEN-teh
At three o'clock	As três	ahs trehs

PORTUGUESE

Portugal, the last world empire to give up the bulk of her possessions, has left "language islands" of Portuguese throughout Africa, Asia, and South America. It is a surprising fact that more people in South America (from Panama south) speak Portuguese than Spanish. In Brazil alone there are more than 100 million people who speak Portuguese.

Portuguese pronunciation characteristics—such as the "zh" sound for *gh* and *j,* and final *m* pronounced "n"—create an interesting linguistic situation: although Portuguese and Spanish are "first-cousin" languages, it is easier for a Portuguese person to understand Spanish than it is for Spanish speakers to understand Portuguese.

PORTUGUESE WORDS
YOU ALREADY KNOW

Portuguese and English have many similar words derived from Latin. With some spelling changes, the Portuguese words become immediately recognizable to English-speakers. Some English words occur in Portuguese, but with different pronunciation and different endings.

Portuguese	English
nação	nation

revolução	revolution
situação	situation
fraternidade	fraternity
liberdade	liberty
sociedade	society
provável	probable
naturalmente	naturally
normalmente	normally
rápidamente	rapidly
evidente	evident
excelente	excellent
presidente	president
monumento	monument
suplemento	supplement

SOME COMMON EXPRESSIONS

Fala português?	FA-la por-too-GEHSS	Do you speak Portuguese?
É americano? (m)	eh ah-meh-ree-KA-no	Are you American?
É americana? (f)	eh ah-meh-ree-KA-na	Are you American?

Até já	ah-TEH zha	Until soon; I'll be right back
Oxalá	oh-sha-LA	I hope so
Saúde!	sa-OO-deh	To your health!
Deus meu!	DEH-ooss MEH-oo	My God!
Até logo	ah-TEH LO-go	Until later
Ótimo	OH-tee-mo	Great
Boa sorte	BO-ah SOR-teh	Good luck
Boa viagem	BO-ah V'YA-gen	Have a good trip
Saudाçãos	sow-da-SOINGS	Regards; Best wishes

Some words of endearment:

É muito simpático (m)	eh MWEEN-toh seem-PA-tee-ko	You are very charming
É muito simpática (f)	eh MWEEN-toh seem-PA-tee-KA	You are very charming
Meu amor	MEH-oo ah-MOR	My love

| Minha vida | MEEN-ya VEE-da | My life |

And otherwise:

Vá-se embora!	VA-seh em-BO-ra	Go away! Get lost!
Vá-se para o diabo!	VA-seh pro dee-AH-bo	Go to the devil!
Malandro	ma-LAHN-dro	Scoundrel

Dutch

Dutch	Nederlands	NAY-der-lahnts

NOTE: In Dutch, *ch* and *g* are pronounced like the *ch* in "Bach"; *ee* is pronounced "ay"; and *u,* rendered as "ů" in the pronunciation column, is pronounced by saying "ee" with the lips held in a tight circle.

Good day	Goeden dag	KHOO-den dakh
Good evening	Goeden avond	KHOO-den AH-vunt
How are you?	Hoe gaat het?	hoo khaht ut
Very well	Heel goed	hayl ghoot
Happy to meet you	Prettig U te ontmoeten	PRET-tukh ů tuh awnt-MOO-tuhn
Good-bye	Dag	dakh
My name	Mijn naam	mayn nahm
Your name	Uw naam	ů nahm

Mr. (and)	Mijnheer (en)	muh-NAYR
Mrs.	Mevrouw	(en) muh-FROW
Miss	Juffrouw	yuh-FROW
Yes	Ja	yah
No; not	Nee; niet	Nay; neet
Excuse me	Pardon	par-DAWN
Please	Alstublieft	ahl-stů-BLEEFT
Thank you	Dank U	dahnk ů
You're welcome	Niet te danken	neet tuh DAHNK-uh
Again	Weer	vayr
Wait	Wachten	VAHKH-tuh
Enough	Genoeg	khuh-NOOKH
Where is	Waar is	vahr iss
the telephone	de telefoon	duh tay-lay-FOHN
the toilet	de W.C.	duh vay-SAY
the airport	de vliegvelt	duh fleekh-felt
the train station	de spoorbaan station	duh SPOHR-bahn sta-S'YON

a bicycle	een fiets	un feets
my baggage	mijn bagage	mayn ba-KHA-juh
the train for ___	de trein naar ___	duh trayn nahr ___
the bus for ___	de bus naar ___	duh boos nahr ___
the boat for ___	de boot naar ___	duh boht nahr ___
What time?	Hoe laat?	hoo laht
Now; not now	Nu; nu niet	nů; nů neet
Later	Later	LAH-ter
A bank	Een bank	un bahnk
A drugstore	Een apotheek	un ah-po-TAYK
A taxi	Een taxi	un TAHK-see
A market	Een markt	un markt
A department store	Een warenhuis	un VA-ruhn-hirs
Far; not far	Ver; niet ver	fair; neet fair
Left; right	Linksaf; rechtsaf	links-AF; rekhts-AF
Here; there	Hier; daar	here; dahr
Open; closed	Open; dicht	OH-pen; dikht

Beautiful	Mooi	mo'ee
How much?	Hoeveel?	hoo-FAYL
Very expensive	Zeer duur	zayr důr
Less expensive	Goedkoper	khoot-KOHP-er
Another color	Nog een kleur	nokh ayn kluhr
Larger	Groter	KHRO-ter
Smaller	Kleiner	KLAY-ner
Hotel	Hotel	ho-TEL
A room (with bath)	Een kamer (met badkammer)	un KA-mer (met BAHT-ka-mar)
Today	Vandaag	vahn-DAHKH
Tomorrow	Morgen	MOHR-khuh
___ days*	___ dagen	___ DA-khuh
What number?	Welk nummer?	velk NOO-mer
Good; not good	Goed; niet goed	khoot; neet khoot

*For numbers see page 86.

A restaurant	Een restaurant	un res-to-RAHN
Soup	Soep	soop
Meat	Vlees	flays
Chicken	Kip	kip
Fish	Vis	fis
Omelet	Omelet	oh-muh-LET
Vegetables	Groenten	KHROON-tuh
Potatoes	Aardappelen	AHRD-ah-puh-len
Bread	Brood	broht
Mineral water	Mineraalwater	mee-nuh-RAHL-VA-ter
Wine or beer	Wijn of bier	wayn of beer
Coffee; tea	Koffee; thee	KAW-fee; tay
Milk	Melk	MEL-uk
Dessert	Dessert	des-SEHR
Delicious	Heerlijk	HAYR-luk
Police	Politie	poh-LEET-see
Doctor	Dokter	dok-ter
Dentist	Tandarts	TAHNT-arts
Sick	Ziek	zeek

Pain	Pijn	payn
Do you understand?	Begrijpt U?	buh-KHRAYPT ů
I don't understand	Ik begrijp het niet	ik buh-KHRAYP ut niet
Slowly	Langzaam	LAHNG-zahm
Possible	Mogelijk	MO-khuh-luk
What is this?	Wat is dit?	vaht iss dit

NUMBERS

0	nul	nool
1	een	ayn
2	twee	tvay
3	drie	dree
4	vier	feer
5	vijf	fayf
6	zes	zess
7	zeven	ZAY-ven
8	acht	ahkht
9	negen	NAY-khen

10	tien	teen
11	elf	EL-uf
12	twaalf	TVAHL-uf
13	dertien	DEHR-teen
14	viertien	FEER-teen
15	vijftien	FAYF-teen
16	zestien	ZESS-teen
17	zeventien	ZAY-vun-teen
18	achttien	AKHT-teen
19	negentien	NAY-khun-teen
20	twintig	TVIN-tukh
21 (etc.)	een en twintig	AYN en TVIN-tukh
30	dertig	DEHR-tukh
40	veertig	FAYR-tukh
50	vijftig	FAYF-tukh
60	zestig	ZESS-tukh
70	zeventig	ZAY-vun-tukh
80	tachtig	TAHKH-tukh
90	negentig	NAY-khun-tukh

100	honderd	HAWN-dert
1,000	duizend	DOY-zent
100,000	honderd duizend	HAWN-dert DOY-zent
1,000,000	miljoen	meel-YOON

For Telling Time

What time is it?	Hoe laat is het?	hoo laht iss het
It's one o'clock	Het is een uur	het iss ayn ůr
It's ten past two	Het is tien na twee	het iss teen na tray
It's half past two	Het is half drie	het iss HA-luf dree
It's ten to ten	Het is tien voor tien	het iss teen for teen
At six o'clock	Om zes uur	ohm zess ůr

DUTCH

Not only is Dutch the language of Holland, but it is also an important world language, especially in commerce. It is spoken in half of Belgium, in Luxembourg, in parts of Africa, on Curaçao and other islands of the Caribbean, in Dutch Guyana, and in the Far East, especially in parts of the former Dutch empire, which included Java and the other islands of Indonesia.

Dutch was one of the first European languages of North America, particularly in New York and New Jersey ("Pennsylvania Dutch" is really German, however). The word *Yankee* comes from the Dutch name Janke, a rural version of Jan. This was first applied pejoratively to Americans by British troops during the American Revolution, implying that the person so named was probably a Dutch settler or peasant.

Many linguists believe that Dutch is a halfway mark between German and English, and an examination of the word list on page 90 would tend to support this opinion. Like English, modern Dutch does not use case endings (as does German), and it tends to adopt international words easily.

The Dutch accent is hard to imitate and frequently difficult to understand. Many words in English and Dutch are close in meaning and spelling, though. It is notable that the Dutch, all things considered, can understand English much more readily than English-speakers can understand Dutch.

Since the Dutch vocabulary is also very close to German, strategists believed that Germans could infiltrate Holland before they began to invade in World War II. But many infiltrators were captured because they failed a simple language test: pronouncing the Dutch words for the number 888 correctly, a task practically impossible for people not born in Holland.

DUTCH WORDS YOU ALREADY KNOW

Many Dutch words are the same as or very similar to their English equivalents. These are simple, short words having to do with basic objects, actions, and needs of daily life.

Dutch	English
arm	arm
bier	beer
best	best
blind	blind
kat	cat
vinger	finger
vlag	flag
handschoen	glove ("hand shoe")
hand	hand
hulp	help
krab	crab
lamp	lamp
land	land
nest	nest
oceaan	ocean

parade	parade
pil	pill
piloot	pilot
pistool	pistol
rat	rat
ring	ring
zee	sea
zend	send
zilver	silver
schip	ship
somer	summer
onder	under
wagon	wagon
water	water
welkom	welcome
west	west
wild	wild
winter	winter
wolf	wolf
werk	work
worm	worm

SOME COMMON EXPRESSIONS

Here are some phrases you will hear in the Netherlands, Belgium, Luxembourg, South Africa, and Dutch possessions or former possessions in the Caribbean and the East Indies.

Spreekt U Nederlands?	spraykt ů NAY-der-lahnts	Do you speak Dutch?
Wat wilt U heben?	vat vilt ů HEB-buh	What will you have?
Op Uw gezondheid!	ohp ů khuh-ZOHNT-hayt	To your health!
Wat gebeurt er?	vat khuh-BUHRT er	What's happening?
Met plezier	met pleh-ZEER	With pleasure
Tot ziens	tawt zeens	So long
Dat is heel vriendelijk van U	dat iss hayl FREEN-duh-luk fahn ů	You are very kind
Goede reis	KHOO-duh rays	Have a good trip
Hartelijke groeten	HAHR-tuh-luk-uh KHROOT-tuh	Best regards

Some words of endearment:

Lieveling	LEE-fuh-ling	Dear; darling
Ik hou van je	ik HOW vahn yuh	I love you

And otherwise:

Lat me met rust!	laht muh met ruhst	Don't bother me!
Idiot	ee-DYOHT	Idiot
Schoft	s'goft	Jerk; Scoundrel

The Scandinavian Languages

The three Scandinavian languages included here, with the exception of various regional accents, resemble one another more closely than do many other languages in contiguous language areas. Words are pronounced approximately as written, although special accents modify the pronunciation of certain letters. You will encounter these accents on signs throughout Sweden, Norway, and Denmark. The special forms are explained in the pronunciation note for each language.

The proximity of Sweden, Norway, and Denmark, and the former union between the last two, has made their languages very similar. Often, if they speak slowly, speakers of any one of the three languages can make themselves understood to speakers of the other two. Swedes, Norwegians, and Danes cannot, however, understand the inhabitants of Iceland, descendants of the great seafarers who explored Greenland and Canada, and perhaps even the Americas as far south as Brazil. Iceland is a true linguistic as well as geographic island. Many who live there must learn foreign languages because very few foreigners speak theirs.

In Sweden, Norway, Denmark, and Greenland (which is Danish-speaking), more than ten percent of the population speaks or understands English. Nevertheless, a foreigner who tries to speak the local language will be received as an especially welcome visitor. However closely these languages resemble one another, it makes for better relations to use words from the appropriate section in each separate country.

An interesting word known to almost all travelers is the general Scandinavian word for "To your health!"—*Skål,* pronounced "skoal." This was originally the word for "skull": in the days of the Vikings, the skulls of the enemy were sometimes modified into drinking bowls. That custom vanished many centuries ago, but the toast itself recalls the days of the ruthless sea raiders.

Some other words from the ancient Norse languages are quite familiar to English-speakers. The words *Tuesday, Wednesday, Thursday,* and *Friday* honor the old Norse gods. Their names, Tiw (god of war and wealth), Wotan or Odin (king of the gods), Thor (god of thunder), and Freya (goddess of beauty), are combined with *dag* ("day"). So in a sense we remember these ancient gods whenever we say, in English, the names of these four days.

| Swedish | Svenska | SVEN-ska |

NOTE: In Swedish, *å* is pronounced "o," *ä* is "eh," *j* is like "y" in "yellow," *ö* is "er" (or "uh"), *sk* before *y* is "sh," *sy* is "s'yew," and *u* is like "ew" in "few." When *en* or *ett* is attached to the end of a noun it means "the"; when it precedes a noun as a separate word, it means "a."

Good day	God dag	goo dahg
Good evening	God afton	good AHF-tohn
How are you?	Hur står det till?	hewr stor deh teel
Very well	Mycket bra	MEW-ket bra
Happy to meet you	Det var roligt	det var ROO-leet
Good-bye	Adjö	ah-YUH
My name	Mitt namn	meet nahmn
Your name	Ert namn	ert nahmn
Mr. (and) Mrs.	Herr (och) Fru	hehrr (oh) frew
Miss	Fröken	frew-ken
Yes	Ja	ya
No; not	Nej; inte	ney; IN-teh
Excuse me	Förlåt	fuhr-LOHT
Please	Var så god	var so good
Thank you	Tack	tahk
You're welcome	Var så god	var so good
Again	Igen	ee-YEN
Wait	Vänta	VEN-ta

Enough	Nog	noog
Where is	Var är	vahr ehr
the telephone	en telefon	ehn teh-leh-FOHN
the toilet	toaletten	too-ah-LEHT-tehn
the airport	flygplatsen	FLEWG-plahts-en
the train station	Järnvägsstationen	jehrn-vehgs-sta-SHOO-nen
a bicycle	en cykel	ehn SEWK-el
my baggage	min väska	meen VESS-ka
the train for ___	tåget til ___	TOH-geht teel ___
the bus for ___	bussen til ___	BEWSS-en teel ___
the boat for ___	båten til ___	BOAT-en teel ___
What time?	Hur dags?	hewr dahks
Now; not now	Nu; inte nu	new; IN-teh new
Later	Senare	SEH-na-reh

A bank	En bank	ehn BAHNK
A drugstore	Ett apotek	et ah-po-TEK
A taxi	En taxi	ehn TAK-see
A market	En affär	ehn af-FEHR
A department store	En stor affär	ehn stoor af-FEHR
Far; not far	Långt; inte långt	lohngt; IN-teh lohngt
Left; right	Vänster; höger	VEHNS-ter; HEW-ger
Here; there	Här; där	hehr; dehr
Open; closed	Öppen; stängd	ERP-pen; stehngd
Beautiful	Vacker	VAK-ker
How much?	Hur mycket?	hewr MEW-ket
Very expensive	Mycket dyr	MEW-ket dewr
Less expensive	Mindre dyr	MEEND-reh dewr
Another color	En annan färg	ehn AN-nahn fehr-ih
Larger	Större	STER-reh
Smaller	Mindre	MEEND-reh

Hotel	Hotel	ho-TEHL
A room (with bath)	Ett rum (med bad)	eht rum (mehd bahd)
Today	I dag	ee dahg
Tomorrow	I morgon	ee MOR-ohn
___ days*	___ dagar	___ DAH-gar
What number?	Vilket nummer?	VEEL-ket NEWM-mer
Good; not good	Gott; inte gott	got; IN-teh got
A restaurant	En restaurang	ehn rehs-ta-RAHNG
Soup	Soppa	SOHP-pa
Meat	Kött	choet
Chicken	Kyckling	CHEWK-leeng
Fish	Fisk	feesk
Omelet	Omelett	oh-meh-let
Vegetables	Grönsaker	GRUHN-sahk-er
Potatoes	Potatis	po-TA-tees

*For numbers see page 101.

Bread	Bröd	bruhd
Mineral water	Mineralvatten	mee-neh-RAL-va-ten
Wine (or) beer	Vin (eller) öl	veen (eller) erl
Coffee; tea	Kaffe; te	KAF-feh; tay
Milk	Mjölk	m'yuhlk
Dessert	Dessert	deh-SEHRT
Delicious	Läcker	LECK-er
Police	Polis	po-LEES
Doctor	Läkare	LEH-ka-reh
Dentist	Tandläkare	TAHND-leh-ka-reh
Sick	Sjuk	shewk
Pain	Smärta	SMEHR-ta
Do you understand?	Förstår ni?	fuhr-STOHR nee?
I don't understand	Jag förstår inte	ja fuhr-STOHR EEN-teh
Slowly	Långsamt	LOHNG-sahmt
Possible	Möjligt	MOY-lit
What is this?	Vad är dette här?	va ehr DEHT-ta here

NUMBERS

The numbers 0 to 12 are especially useful and should be commited to memory.

0	noll	nool
1	ett	eht
2	två	t'vo
3	tre	treh
4	fyra	FEW-ra
5	fem	fehm
6	sex	sex
7	sju	shew
8	åtta	OH-ta
9	nio	NEE-yo
10	tio	TEE-yo
11	elva	EHL-va
12	tolv	tohlv
13	tretton	TREH-tohn
14	fjorton	FEWR-tohn
15	femton	FEHM-tohn
16	sexton	SEX-tohn

17	sjutton	SHEW-tohn
18	arton	AHR-tohn
19	nitton	NEE-tohn
20	tjugo	SHEW-guh
21 (etc.)	tjugoett	shew-go-EHT
30	trettio	TREH-t'yo
40	fyrtio	FUR-t'yo
50	femtio	FEM-t'yo
60	sextio	SEX-t'yo
70	sjuttio	SHOO-t'yo
80	åttio	OH-t'yo
90	nittio	NEE-t'yo
100	hundra	HUN-dra
1,000	tusen	TEW-sehn
100,000	hundra tusen	HUN-dra TEW-sehn
1,000,000	miljon	mill-YOHN

For Telling Time

"Half past" is expressed by saying halfway to the *next* hour.

What time is it?	Hur mycket är klockan?	hew MEW-keh eh KLO-kan
It's one o'clock	Kpockan är ett	KLO-kan eh eht
Half past one (halfway to two)	Halv två	halv tvo
It's two o'clock	Klockan är två	KLO-kan eh tvo

SOME COMMON EXPRESSIONS

Hej	Hey	Hello; Good-bye
Talar Ni Svenska?	TA-lahr nee SVEN-ska	Do you speak Swedish?
Var är Ni från?	var eh nee frohn	Where are you from?
Välkommen	VEL-ko-men	Welcome
Stig in	steeg in	Come in
Skål!	skoal	To your health!
Tycker Du om det?	TEW-keh dew ohm deh	Do you like it?

Tack för maten*	tahk fuhr MA-ten	Thanks for the food
Lycka til	lew-keh til	Good luck
Är det allt?	Ehr deh alt	Is that all?
Inte sänt?	IN-teh sent	Isn't it so?
Vad står på?	vahd stor po	What's the matter?
Var så god	var so good	Go ahead; You first
Skynda på	SHEWN-da po	Hurry up
Så här	so hair	This way
Här är det	hair ehr deh	Here it is

And for a more romantic mood:

| Du är så snäl | dew air so snel | You are charming |
| Jag tycker mycket om Dig | yahg TEW-ker MEW-ket ohm day | I like you very much |

Or, for other circumstances:

| Gå din väg! | Go deen VAYG | Go away! |

*This is the common polite phrase to say after a meal.

Norwegian	Norsk	norsk

NOTE: In Norwegian, *å* is pronounced "o"; *j* is pronounced like the "y" in "yellow"; *ø* is pronounced "ew"; and *y* is pronounced by saying "ee" with the lips held in a tight circle. When *en* or *et* is attached to the end of a noun, it means "the"; when *en* or *et* precedes a noun as a separate word, it means "a."

Good day	God dag	goo dahg
Good evening	God kveld	goo kvehl
How are you?	Hvordan står det til?	vohr-DAHN stor deh teel
Very well	Bra	bra
Happy to meet you	Koselig å møte Dem	KOO-seh-lig oh mew-te dehm
Good-bye	Farvel	far-VEHL
My name	Mitt navn	meet nahvn
Your name	Deres navn	DEHR-es nahvn
Mr. (and) Mrs.	Herr (og) Fru	hehr (oh) frew
Miss	Frøken	FREW-ken

Yes	Ja	ya
No; not	Nei; ikke	nay; ICK-keh
Excuse me	Unnskyld	EWN-shewl
Please	Vennligst	VEHN-leegst
Thank you	Takk	tahk
You're welcome	Ingen årsak	EEN-gen OR-sahk
Again	Igjen	ee-YEN
Wait	Vent	vehnt
Enough	Nok	nohk
Where is	Hvor er	vor ehr
the telephone	telefonen	teh-leh-FOHN-en
the toilet	klosettet	klo-SEHT-tet
the airport	flyplassen	FLEE-plahs-sen
the train station	jernbanestasj-onen	jehrn-ba-neh-sta-SHO-nen
a bicycle	en sykkel	ehn SICK-kel
my luggage	bagasjen min	ba-GAHSH-en meen
the train for ____	toget til ____	TOHG-eh teel ____

the bus for ____	bussen til ____	BEWS-sen teel ____
the boat for ____	båten til ____	boat-en teel ____
What time?	Hvilken tid, når?	VEEL-ken teed, nohr
Now; not now	Nå; ikke nå	no; ICK-keh no
Later	Senere	SEHN-eh-reh
A bank	En bank	ehn bahnk
A drugstore	Et apotek	eht ah-po-TEK
A taxi	En bil	ehn beel
A market	Et torg	eht torg
A department store	En stor forretning	ehn stoor for-REHT-neeng
Far; not far	Langt; ikke langt	lahngt; ICK-keh lahngt
Left; right	Venstre; høyre	VEHNS-treh; HEW-reh
Here; there	Her; der	hehr; dehr
Open; closed	Åpent; lukket	OHP-ent; LEWK-ket
Beautiful	Vakker	VAHK-ker

How much?	Hvor meget?	vohr **MEH**-get
Very expensive	Veldig dyrt	**VEHL**-dig durt
Less expensive	Mindre dyrt	**MEEN**-dreh durt
Another color	En annen farge	ehn **AHN**-en **FAHRG**-eh
Larger	Større	**STEW**-reh
Smaller	Mindre	**MEEN**-dreh
Hotel	Hotel	ho-**TEHL**
A room (with bath)	Et vaerelse (med bad)	eht **VEHR**-el-seh (meh bahd)
Today	I dag	ee dag
Tomorrow	I morgen	ee **MOR**-en
____ days*	____ dager	____ **DA**-gher
What number?	Hvilket nummer?	**VEEL**-ket **NUM**-mer
Good; not good	Godt; ikke godt	got; **ICK**-keh got
A restaurant	En restaurant	ehn res-tew-**RAHNG**
Soup	Suppe	**SEWP**-peh

*For numbers see page 110.

Meat	Kjøtt	shewt
Chicken	Kylling	SHEWL-leeng
Fish	Fisk	feesk
Omelet	Omelett	oh-meh-LET
Vegetables	Grønasaker	GREWN-sahk-er
Potatoes	Poteter	poo-TEHT-er
Bread	Brød	bruh
Mineral water	Mineralvann	mee-neh-RAHL-vahn
Wine (or) beer	Vin (eller) øl	veen (EL-ler) ewl
Coffee; tea	Kaffe; te	KAHF-feh; teh
Milk	Melk	mehlk
Dessert	Dessert	deh-SEHR
Delicious	Delikat	deh-lee-KAHT
Police	Politi	poo-lee-TEE
Doctor	Lege	LEH-geh
Dentist	Tannlege	TAHN-leh-geh
Sick	Syk	sewk

Pain	Smerte	SMEHR-teh
Do you understand?	Forstår De?	fohr-STOR dee
I don't understand	Jeg forstår ikke	yay fohr-STOR ICK-keh
Slowly	Langsomt	LAHNG-sohmt
Possible	Mulig	MEW-lee
What is this?	Hva er dette?	va ehr DET-teh

NUMBERS

0	null	nool
1	en	ehn
2	to	too
3	tre	treh
4	fire	FEE-reh
5	fem	fehm
6	seks	sex
7	sju	shew
8	åtte	OHT-teh

9	ni	nee
10	ti	tee
11	elleve	EH-leh-veh
12	tolv	tohl
13	tretten	TRET-ten
14	fjorten	FYOOR-ten
15	femten	FEHM-ten
16	seksten	SAY-sen
17	sytten	SOOT-ten
18	atten	AHT-ten
19	nitten	NIT-ten
20	tjue	T'YEW-eh
21 (etc.)	tjueen	t'yew-eh-EHN
30	tretti	TRET-tee
40	førti	FUR-tee
50	femti	FEHM-tee
60	seksti	SEX-tee
70	sytti	SOOT-tee
80	åtti	OHT-tee
90	nitti	NIT-tee
100	hundre	HEWN-dreh

1,000	tusen	TEW-sehn
100,000	hundre tusen	HEWN-dreh TEW-sehn
1,000,000	million	meel-YOHN

For Telling Time

"Half past" is expressed by saying halfway to the *next* hour.

What time is it?	Hva er klokken?	va ehr KLO-ken
It is one o'clock	Den er en	dehn ehr ehn
Half past one (halfway to two)	Halv to	hahl too
Five to two	Fem på to	fehm po too
Two o'clock	Klokken to	KLO-ken too

SOME COMMON EXPRESSIONS

Hei	hey	Hello
Snakker De norsk?	SNA-ker dee norsk	Do you speak Norwegian?
Velkommen	vel-KO-men	Welcome
Kom inn	kom in	Come in

Skål!	skoal	To your health!
Liker De den?	LEEK-er dee dehn	Do you like it?
Takk for maten*	takh for MA-ten	Thanks for the food
Lykke til	LEWK-keh teel	Good luck
Er det alt?	air de alt	Is that all?
Ikke sant?	ICK-eh sahnt	Isn't it so?
Hva er det i veien?	hva er deh ee VEY-en	What's the matter?
Skynd Dem	shin dem	Hurry up
Likesom det	lee-keh-SOM deh	Like that
Her er den	hair er dehn	Here it is
Gå din vei!	go deen vey	Go away!

Danish	Dansk	dahnsk

NOTE: In Danish, æ is said as "eh," ø sounds like "er" with the "r" subordinated, sk is pronounced "sh," and y is pronounced by saying "ee" with the lips in a tight circle, as indicated by "e̊" in the

*This is the common polite phrase to say after a meal.

phonetic column. Danish has "silent" letters as well, as suggested in the third column. When *en* or *et* is a suffix, attached to the end of a noun, it means "the"; when *en* or *et* precedes a noun as a separate word, it means "a."

Good day	God dag	goo-day
Good evening	God aften	godh AFT-en
How are you?	Hvordan har De det?	vorh-DAHN hahr dee deh
Very well	Meget godt	MAY-et goth
Happy to meet you	Det var morsomt	deh var mor-SAHMT
Good-bye	Farvel	fahr-VEHL
My name	Mit navn	meet nown
Your name	Deres navn	DEHR-ehs nown
Mr. (and) Mrs.	Herre (og) Fru	HEHR (oh) FROO
Miss	Frøken	FRER-ken
Yes	Ja	ya
No; not	Nej; ikke	nay; ICK-eh
Excuse me	Undskyld mig	OON-skewl my

Please	Vær venlig	vehr VEHN-lee
Thank you	Tak	tahk
You're welcome	Du er velkommen	doo eh vel-KO-men
Again	Igen	ee-GEN
Wait	Vent	vehnt
Enough	Nok	nohk
Where is	Hvor er	vohr ehr
the telephone	telefonen	teh-leh-FOHN-en
the toilet	toilettet	twa-LEHT-edh
the airport	lufthavnen	LOOFT-how-nen
the train station	tog stationen	toh stah-SHOHN-en
a bicycle	en cykel	ehn SEWK-el
my baggage	min bagage	meen ba-GAHZH
the train for ____	toget til ____	TOH-edh teel ____
the bus for ____	bussen til ____	BOOS-en teel ____

the boat for	båden til	BO-then teel

What time?	Hvad tid?	va teedh
Now; not now	nu; ikke nu	noo; ICK-eh noo
Later	Senere	SEHN-eh-reh
A bank	En bank	ehn bahnk
A drugstore	Et apotek	eht ah-po-TEK
A taxi	En taxa	ehn TAHK-sa
A market	Et torv	eht torv
A department store	Et stormagasin	eht stor-ma-ga-ZEEN
Far; not far	Langt; ikke langt	lahngt; ICK-ch lahngt
Left; right	Venstre; højre	VEHN-streh; HOY-reh
Here; there	Her; der	hehr; dehr
Open; closed	Åben; lukket	OH-ben; LOOK-ket
Beautiful	Smuk	smook
How much?	Hvor meget?	vohr MA-edh
Very expensive	Meget dyrt	MAY-et dewrt

Less expensive	Mindre dyrt	MEEN-dreh dewrt
Another color	En anden farve	ehn EHN-den FAHR-veh
Larger	Større	STER-reh
Smaller	Mindre	MEEN-dreh
Hotel	Hotel	ho-TEHL
A room (with bath)	Et værelse (med bad)	eht VEH-rel-seh (medh badh)
Today	I dag	ee day
Tomorrow	I morgen	ee mohrn
___ days*	___ dage	___ DAY-heh
What number?	Hvad nummer?	vadh NOO-mer
Good; not good	Godt; ikke godt	got; ICK-eh got
A restaurant	En restaurant	ehn res-toh-RAHNG
Soup	Suppe	SOO-peh
Meat	Kød	kerdh

*For numbers see page 119.

Chicken	Kylling	KEW-leeng
Fish	Fisk	fisk
Omelet	Omelet	oh-meh-LET
Vegetables	Grønsager	GRERN-say-er
Potatoes	Kartofler	kar-TOHF-ler
Bread	Brød	brerdh
Mineral water	Mineralvand	mee-nee-RAHL-vahn
Wine (or) beer	Vin (eller) øl	veen (EL-ler) erl
Coffee; tea	Kaffe; the	KAF-feh; tea
Milk	Mælk	mehlk
Dessert	Dessert	des-SAIR
Delicious	Delikat	deh-lee-KAHT
Police	Politi	po-lee-TEE
Doctor	Dokter	DOHK-tehr
Dentist	Tandlæge	TAN-leh-yeh
Sick	Syg	sĕe
Pain	Smerte	SMEHR-teh
Do you understand?	Forstår De?	for-STOR dee

I don't understand	Jeg forstår ikke	yay for-STOR ICK-eh
Slowly	Langsomt	LAHNG-sohmt
Possible	Muligt	MOOL-eet
What is this?	Hvad er dette?	vadh ehr DET-teh

NUMBERS

0	nul	nool
1	een	ehn
2	to	too
3	tre	treh
4	fire	feer
5	fem	fehm
6	seks	sex
7	syv	soo
8	otte	OH-teh
9	ni	nee
10	ti	tee
11	elleve	EHL-veh

12	tolv	tohl
13	tretten	TREH-ten
14	fjorten	FYOHR-d'n
15	femten	FEHM-d'n
16	seksten	SICE-d'n
17	sytten	SOO-d'n
18	atten	EH-d'n
19	nitten	NEE-d'n
20	tyve	TEW-veh
21 (etc.)	een og tyve (literally, "one-and-twenty")	ehn oh TEW-veh
30	tredive	TREH-veh
40	fyrre	fur
50	halvtreds	hahl-TRESS
60	tres	tress
70	halvfjerds	hahl-F'YAHSS
80	firs	feers
90	halvfems	hahl-FEHMS
100	hundrede	HOON-reh-deh

1,000	tusind	TOO-sind
100,000	hundrede tusind	HOON-reh-deh TOO-sind
1,000,000	million	meel-YOHN

For Telling Time

"Half past" is expressed by saying halfway to the *next* hour.

What time is it?	Hvad er klokken?	va ehr KLO-ken?
It's one o'clock	Klokken een	KLO-ken ett
Half past one (halfway to two)	Halv to	hahl too
Two o'clock	Klokken to	KLO-ken too

SOME COMMON EXPRESSIONS

Hej	hi	Hello
Taler De dansk?	TA-ler dee dahnsk	Do you speak Danish?
Velkommen	VEL-ko-men	Welcome
Kom ind	kom in	Come in

Skål!	skoal	To your health!
Kan du lide det?	kehn doo LEE deh	Do you like it?
Tak for mad*	tahk for madh	Thanks for the food
Held og lykke	hel oh LEW-keh	Good luck
Er det alt?	er deh alt	Is that all?
Ikke sandt?	ICK-eh sahnt	Isn't it so?
Hvad er der i vejen?	hvahd air dair ee VY-en	What's the matter?
Værsågod	VEHR-so-good	Go ahead; You first
Skynd Dem	skewn dem	Hurry up
Ligesom det	LEE-som deh	Like that
Her er den	hair air dehn	Here it is
Gå din vej!	go din vey	Go away!

And for special occasions:

Hvornår kan vi mødes igen?	Vor-NOR kan vee MUH-dehs EE-gen	When can I see you again?

*This is the common polite phrase to say after a meal.

RUSSIAN

Russian	по-русский	pa-ROO-skee
Good day	Добрый день	DOH-bree d'yen'
Good evening	Добрый вечер	DOH-bree v'yeh-cher
How are you?	Как вы пожи-ваете?	kahk vee pa-zhee-VA-yeh-t'yeh
Very well	Очень хоро-шо	OH-chen' ha-ra-SHO
Happy to meet you	Очень рад (man speaker)	OH-chen rahd
	Очень рада (woman speaker)	OH-chen' ra-da
Good bye	До свидания	da svee-DA-n'ya
My name	Моё имя	ma-YO EEM-ya
Your name	Ваше имя	VA-sheh EEM-ya

Mr. (citizen of USSR)	Гражданин*	grazh-da-NEEN
Mrs.; Miss (citizen of USSR)	Гражданка*	grazh-DAHN-ka
Yes	Да	da
No; not	Нет; не	n'eyt; n'yeh
Excuse me	Извините	iz-vee-NEE-t'yeh
Please	Пожалуйста	pa-ZHAHL-sta
Thank you	Спасибо	spa-SEE-ba
You're welcome	Не за чта	N'YEH za shta
Again	Опять	ah-p'YAHT'
Wait	Ждать	zh'daht'
Enough	Довольна	do-VOHL-na
Where is	Где	gd'yeh
the telephone	телефон	teh-leh-FOHN
the toilet	туалет	twa-LET
the airport	аэропорт	ah-eh-ro-PORT

* The words for "Mr.," "Mrs.," and "Miss," applied to foreigners, are the old pre-revolution forms of "Lord" and "Lady" — *Gospodin* and *Gospozha*.

the train station	вокзал	vohk-ZAHL
the subway	метро	met-RO
my baggage	мой багаж	moy ba-GAHZ
the train for ____	поезд до ____	po-YEZD doh ____
the bus for ____	автобус до ____	aff-TOH-boos doh ____
the boat for ____	лодка до ____	LOHT-ka doh ____
What time?	Который час?	ka-TOH-ree chahss
Now; not now	Теперь; не теперь	t'yeh-P'YEHR; n'yeh t'yeh-P'YEHR
Later	Позже	POHZ-zheh
A bank	Банк	bahnk
A drugstore	Аптека	ahp-T'YEH-ka
A taxi stand	Стоянка такси	Stahn-ka tahk-SEE
A market	Рынок	REE-nock
A department store	Универмаг	oo-nee-vehr-MAHG

Far; not far	Далеко; не далеко	da-l'yeh-KO; n'yeh da-l'yeh-KO
Left; right	Левый; правый	L'YEH-vee; PRA-vee
Here; there	Здесь; там	z'd'yess; tahm
Open; closed	Открыто; закрыто	aht-KREE-ta; za-KREE-ta
Beautiful	Красиво	kra-SEE-va
How much?	Сколько?	SKOHL-ka
Very expensive	Очень дорого	OH-chen dara-GO
Less expensive	Не так дорого	n'yeh tahk dara-GO
Another color	Другого цвета	droo-GO-vo ts'VYEH-ta
Larger	Больше	BOHL-sheh
Smaller	Меньше	M'YEN-sheh
Hotel	Гостиница	ga-STEE-neet-sa
A room (with bath)	Комната (с ванной)	KOHM-na-ta (s'bahn-NOY)
Today	Сегодня	seh-VOHD-n'ya

Tomorrow	Завтра	ZAHV-tra
____ days*	____ дня	____ dn'ya
What number?	Какой номер?	ka-KOY NO-mer
Good; not good	Хорошо; не хорошо	ha-ra-SHO; n'yeh ha-ra-SHO
A restaurant	Ресторан	res-ta-RAHN
Soup	Суп	soop
Meat	Мясо	M'YA-sa
Chicken	Курица	KOO-reet-sa
Fish	Рыба	REE-ba
Omelet	Яичница	YA-ICH-nit-sa
Vegetables	Овощи	OH-vosh-shee
Potatoes	Картошка	kar-TOHSH-ka
Bread	Хлеб	khleb
Mineral water	Минеральная вода	mee-neh-RAL-nee-ya va-DA
Wine (or) beer	Вино (или) пиво	vee-NO (EE-lee) PEE-va
Coffee; tea	Кофе; чай	KO-feh; chai
Milk	Молоко	ma-la-KO

*For numbers see page 129.

Dessert	Сладкое	SLAHT-ko-yeh
Delicious (very good)	Очень хорошо	OH-chen ha-ra-SHO
Police	Милиция	mee-LEET-see-ya
Doctor	Врач	VRAH'ch
Dentist	Зубной врач	zoob-NOY vrah'ch
Sick	Больной	bahl-noy
Pain	Боль	bohl
Do you understand?	Понимаете?	pa-nee-MA-eht-yeh
I don't understand	Не понимаю	n'yeh pa-nee-MA-yoo
Slowly	Медленно	M'YED-leh-na
Possible	Можно	MOHZH-na
What is this?	Что это?	ch'toh ET-ta

NUMBERS

The Arabic numerals are used in Russian. The words for 1 through 10 are given in Cyrillic and spelled phonetically. For numbers 11 and over, only the phonetic spelling is given.

0	ноль	nohl
1	один	ah-DEEN
2	два	d'va
3	три	tree
4	четыре	cheh-TEE-reh
5	пять	p'yaht
6	шесть	shest
7	семь	s'yem
8	восемь	VO-s'yem
9	девять	D'YEH-v'yaht
10	десять	D'YEH-s'yaht
11		ah-dee-NA-tsaht
12		d'veh-NA-tsaht
13		tree-NA-tsaht
14		cheh-TEER-na-tsaht

15	p'yaht-NA-tsaht
16	shess-NA-tsaht
17	s'yem-NA-tsaht
18	vo-s'yem-NA-tsaht
19	deh-v'yaht-NA-tsaht
20	DVA-tsaht
21 (etc.)	DVA-tsaht ah-DEEN
30	TREE-tsaht
40	SO-rock
50	p'yaht-deh-s'YAHT
60	shest-deh-s'YAHT
70	s'YEM-deh-s'yaht
80	VO-s'yem-deh-s'yaht

90	deh-v'ya-NO-sto
100	sto
1,000	TIH-s'ya-cha
100,000	sto-TIH-s'ya-cha
1,000,000	meel-YOHN

For Telling Time

Only the phonetic spellings of the Russian are given here.

What time is it?	ka-TOH-ree chahss
One o'clock	chahss (hour)
Two o'clock	dva chah-SA (from two to four, "o'clock" is chah-SA)
Five o'clock	p'yaht chah-SOV (from five to twelve, "o'clock" is chah-SOV)

Time toward the *next* hour can be indicated in minutes of half-hours, with the *coming* hour taking an ending in *-ova*.

Twenty past one	DVA-tsaht mee-NOOT v'ta-RO-va (twenty *toward* two)
Half past one	pa-lo-VEE-na v'ta-RO-va (literally "half *to* two")

RUSSIAN

Russian is spoken over the largest continuous section of the earth's surface. It is the official language of the multilanguage Soviet Union and is spoken by at least 200 million people. It is familiar to other millions in countries such as Poland, Yugoslavia, Bulgaria, and Czechoslovakia, all of whose languages are even closer to Russian than the Latin languages are to each other. Russian is also one of the six official languages used at the United Nations, and is of increasing importance as a world language.

The Russian Cyrillic alphabet (named for the medieval St. Cyril) has seven more letters than our alphabet. The following brief explanation, aided by comparison of the middle and right columns in the preceding vocabulary section, will help you pronounce words on Russian street and shop signs.

The letters *a, e, k, m, o, t*, and з (*z*) sound and look more or less the same in both languages. For the other letters, see below: the Russian letter is on

the left of the equals sign, the Roman letter or
equivalent English sound combination on the right.

б	=	b
в	=	v
г	=	g
д	=	d
ё	=	yo
ж	=	zh
и	=	i (ee)
й	=	y
л	=	l
н	=	n
п	=	p
р	=	r
с	=	s
у	=	u (oo)
ф	=	f
х	=	h, kh
ц	=	ts, tz
ч	=	ch
ш	=	sh
щ	=	shch

ъ	=	(mute)
ы	=	i (ih)
ь	=	serves to "soften" previous letter
э	=	e
ю	=	yu
я	=	ya

RUSSIAN WORDS YOU ALREADY KNOW

Most Russian words used in English refer to food or politics: *borscht, blini, samovar* ("self-boiling"), *vodka* ("little water"), *Kremlin* ("the enclosed"), *tovarisch* (comrade), and *soviet* (from the word for "advice"). Russian shares a number of recognizable Greek-origin words with English, such as *kosmos* (space), *kosmonaft* (cosmonaut), *telefon, teknologhia, telegramma,* and *atomnaya bomba.*

Among words in English that, interestingly, came from Russian via other cultures is *bistro,* adopted into French from *bistra* (Russian for "Hurry up!"), a word used by the invading Cossack horsemen in Paris after Waterloo to urge café owners to speed up their service. Another is *hooligan,* from the name of a tumultuous Irish family in a play Czar Nicholas II had seen as a young man in London. Because of his frequent retelling of the plot, the word *hooligan* was adopted into Russian; it referred to a fractious and undesirable vagabond.

Russians have always admired the color red, even before it became associated with politics. This probably stems from the color's being associated with life and action in a land covered by snow and bleak skies during much of the year. The best room in a house used to have a section of honor, the "red corner," which held the finest furnishings. A pretty girl was a "red girl," and the great central square in Moscow was called "Red Square" long before the Revolution.

Recently two Russian words have gained world-wide attention: *perestroika,* which means "restructuring" (to the advantage of international relations, one hopes), and *glasnost,* translated as "openness." It comes from the Russian word for "voice" *(glas)* and means basically the "ability to give voice"—in other words, freedom to speak, certainly a greatly desired aim of the peoples of our planet.

SOME COMMON EXPRESSIONS

go-vo-REET-yeh pa ROOS-kee	Do you speak Russian?
vee am-er-ree-KA-netz	Are you American? (m)
vee am-er-ree-KAHN-ka	Are you American? (f)

vee ahn-glee-CHA-nin	Are you English? (m)
vee ahn-glee-CHAHN-ka	Are you English? (f)
DOH-bra po-zha-la-VAHT	Welcome
vye-DEE t'yeh	Come in
CH'TOH-vee	Really?
preh-KRA-sna	Great!
za VA-sha z'da-RO-v'yah	To your health!
DOH-bra-va poo-TEE	Have a good trip
meer MEE-roo	Peace* to the world
uy-DEET-t'yeh	Go away!

Some words of endearment:

da-ra-GOY	Dear (m)
da-ra-GA-ya	Dear (f)
MEE-len-kee	Darling (m)
MEE-len-kasya	Darling (f)

*Mir, Russian for "peace," has two other meanings, "village council" and "world," depending on how it is used.

And otherwise—but use with caution!

oos-pa-KOY-t'yes	Take it easy
doo-RAK	Fool
ee-d'YOT	Idiot

Serbo-Croatian

Serbo-Croatian	Srpsko-Hravtski	SRPS-ko-hra-VAHT-skee

NOTE: In some cases, Serbian and Croatian terms differ. Throughout, "SR" indicates the Serbian word or phrase, and "CR" the Croatian. Travelers are advised to use the Serbian term in Serbia and the Croatian in Croatia. In both Serbian and Croatian, *c* is pronounced as "ts," *č* as "ch," *j* as "y" as in "yellow," *š* as "sh," and *ž* as "zh."

Good day	Dobar dan	DOH-bar dahn
Good evening	Dobro veče	DOHB-ro VEH-chehr
How are you?	Kako ste?	KA-ko steh
Very well	Dobro	DOH-bro
Happy to meet you	Drago mi je vas upoznati	DRA-go mee yeh vas oo-pohz-NA-tee
Good-bye	Zbogom	Z'BO-gohm

My name	Moje ime	MO-yeh EE-meh
Your name	Vaše ime	VA-sheh EE-meh
Mr. (and) Mrs.	Gospodin (i) Gospodja	gohs-PO-deen (ee) GOHS-po-ja
Miss	Gospodjica	GOHS-po-jeet-sa
Yes	Da	da
No; not	Ne; nije	neh; NEE-yeh
Excuse me	Izvinite (SR) Oprostite (CR)	eez-VEE-nee-teh o-pro-STEE-teh
Please	Molim	MO-leem
Thank you	Hvala	H'FA-la
You're welcome	Molim	MO-leem
Again	Opet	OHP-eht
Wait	Čekajte	CHEH-ky-teh
Enough	Dosta	DOHS-ta
Where is	Gdje	g'jeh
the telephone	telefon	teh-LEH-fohn

the toilet	toaleta	toh-ah-LEH-ta
the airport	aerodrom	ah-EHR-o-drohm
the train station	željeznička stanica	ZHEH-lyehz-neech-ka STA-neet-sa
a bicycle	bicikl	bee-TSEE-kel
my baggage	moja prtljaga	MO-ya pirt-LYAH-ga
the train for ___	vlak za ___	v'lahk za ___
the bus for ___	autobus za ___	ow-TOH-boos za ___
the boat for ___	brod za ___	brohd za ___
What time?	Koliko sati?	KO-lee-ko SA-tee
Now; not now	Sada; nije sada	SAHD-a; NEE-yeh SAHD-a
Later	Kasnije	KAHSS-nee-yeh
A bank	Banka	BAHN-ka
A drugstore	Apoteka	ahp-o-TEH-ka

A taxi	Taksi	TAHK-see
A market	Tržnica	TERZH-nee-tsa
A department store	Robna kuča	ROHB-na KOO-cha
Far; not far	Daleko; nije daleko	da-LEH-ko; NEE-yeh da-LEH-ko
Left	Levo (SR) Lijevo (CR)	LEH-vo lee-YEH-vo
Right	Desno	DEHS-no
Here	Ovde (SR) Ovdje (CR)	OHV-deh OHV-yeh
There	Tamo	TA-mo
Open; closed	Otvoreno; zatvoreno	oht-VO-reh-no; zaht-VO-reh-no
Beautiful	Lepo (SR) Lijepo (CR)	LEH-po lee-YEH-po
How much?	Koliko?	ko-LEE-ko
Very expensive	Vrlo skupo	vrlo SKOOP-o

Less expensive	Jeftinije	YEHF-tin-ee-yeh
Another color	Druga boja	DROO-ga BO-ya
Larger	Veči	VEH-chee
Smaller	Manji	MAHN-yee
Hotel	Hotel	(pronounced as in English)
A room (and bath)	Soba (i kupaonica)	SO-ba (ee koo-PA-o-nee-tsa)
Today	Danas	DAHN-ahs
Tomorrow	Sutra	SOO-tra
____ days*	____ dana	____ DA-na
What number?	Koji broj?	KO-yee broy
Good; not good	Dobro; nije dobro	DOH-bro; NEE-yeh DOH-bro
A restaurant	Restoran	reh-STO-rahn
Soup	Juha	YOO-ha
Meat	Meso	MEH-so
Chicken	Kokica	ko-KEE-tsa

*For numbers see page 144.

Fish	Riba	REE-ba
Eggs	Jaja	YA-ya
Vegetables	Povrče	POHVR-cheh
Potatoes	Krumpir	KROOM-peer
Bread	Hleb (SR)	h'leb
	Kruh (CR)	krooh
Mineral water	Mineralna voda	mee-nee-RAHL-na VO-da
Wine (or) beer	Vino (ili) pivo	VEE-no (EE-lee) PEE-vo
Coffee; tea	Kava; čaj	KA-va; chai
Milk	Mleko (SR)	MLEH-ko
	Mlijeko (CR)	mlee-YEH-ko
Dessert	Poslastice	POHZ-lahss-tee-tse
Very good	Vrlo dobro	vr'lo DOH-bro
Police	Milicija	mee-LEET-see-ya
Doctor	Lekar	LEH-kar
Dentist	Zubni lekar	ZOOB-nee LEH-kar

Sick	Bolestan	BO-leh-stahn
Pain	Bol	bohl
Do you understand?	Da li Vi razumete? (SR) Da li Vi razumjete? (CR)	da lee vee ra-ZOO-meh-teh da lee vee ra-ZOOM-yeh-teh
I don't understand	Ja ne razumem (SR) Ja ne razumjem (CR)	ya neh ra-ZOO-mehm ya neh ra-ZOOM-yehm
Slowly	Sporo	SPOH-ro
Possible	Moguče	MO-goo-cheh
What is this?	Šta je ovo? (SR) Što je ovo? (CR)	shta yeh O-vo shto yeh O-vo

NUMBERS

0	nula	NOO-la
1	jedan	YEH-dahn
2	dva	d'va

3	tri	tree
4	četri	CHET-ree
5	pet	peht
6	šest	shehst
7	sedam	SEH-dahm
8	osam	O-sahm
9	devet	DEH-vet
10	deset	DEH-set
11	jedanajest	YEH-da-nah-yest
12	dvanajest	DVA-nah-yest
13	trinajest	TREE-nah-yest
14	četrnajest	CHETR'-nah-yest
15	petnajest	PET-nah-yest
16	šestnajest	SHESH-nah-yest
17	sedamnajest	SEH-dahm-nah-yest
18	osamnajest	OH-sahm-nah-yest
19	devetnajest	DEH-veht-nah-yest

20	dvadeset	DVA-deh-set
21 (etc.)	dvadeset i jedan (etc.)	DVA-deh-set ee YEH-dahn
30	trideset	TREE-deh-set
40	četrdeset	chetr'-DEH-set
50	pedeset	p'yeh-DEH-set
60	šezdeset	shez-DEH-set
70	sedamdeset	seh-dahm-DEH-set
80	osamdeset	oh-sehm-DEH-set
90	devedeset	DEH-veh-DEH-set
100	sto	sto
1,000	hiljada	HEEL-ya-da
100,000	sto hiljada	sto HEEL-ya-da
1,000,000	milion	mil-ee-YOHN

For Telling Time

| What time is it? | Koliko je sati? | ko-LEE-ko yeh SA-tee |
| Two o'clock | Dva sata | dva SA-ta |

Two-ten	Dva i deset	dva ee DEH-set
Half past two	Dva i po	dva ee po
Ten to three	Deset do tri	DEH-set doh tree
Three o'clock	Tri sata	tree SA-ta

SERBO-CROATIAN

The name Yugoslavia implies the land of the southern Slavs. Its language, Serbo-Croatian, unites the two main elements of the population. Serbs and Croatians speak versions of a language resembling Russian, but they use different alphabets. The Serbian alphabet is written in Cyrillic letters, as is Russian, while Croatian uses the Latin alphabet (to the relief of West European and English-speaking tourists). In addition, as noted previously, some of their specific words and expressions differ as well. Many signs and papers in Yugoslavia are written in both alphabets: Cyrillic for Serbs, Roman for Croatians. Still another language, Slovene, is widely spoken, but a Serbo-Croatian vocabulary is sufficient to express your needs and wishes.

In ancient times the Roman Empire encompassed what is now Yugoslavia. A trace of Rome is still evident in the national currency, the dinar, whose name recalls the Roman *denarius,* the coin once paid to Roman legionaries. When Yugoslavia was part of the old Austro-Hungarian Empire, German was widely spoken in the northwest. Now, however, Serbo-Croatian is dominant to the point that even the official name of a large northern port city was changed. It used to be called Fiume, the Italian for "river"; its new name is Rijeka, which also means "river," but in Serbo-Croatian.

Serbo-Croatian words are relatively easy to pronounce, except when a number of consonants run together. Take the word for "Serbo-Croatian," for instance, *Srpsko-Hrvatski.* Insert apostrophes— *S'r'p'sko H'r'vatski*—and you will find it easier to pronounce, although this spelling seems unusual for an English-speaker.

SOME COMMON EXPRESSIONS

Zdravo	ZDRA-vo	Hello
Govorite li Srpsko-Hrvatski?	Go-VOR-ee-teh lee SRPS-ko-hra-VAHT-skee	Do you speak Serbo-Croatian?
Dobro došli	DOH-bro DOSH-lee	Welcome
Udjite	OO-djee-teh	Come in
U vaše zdravlje!	oo VA-sheh ZDRAHV-l'yeh	To your health!

Da li volite?	da lee VO-lee-teh	Do you like it?
Sretno	SRET-no	Good luck
Da li to je sve?	da lee toh yeh s'veh	Is that all?
Zar nije?	zar NEE-yah	Isn't it so?
Što je?	shto yeh	What's the matter?
Izvolite	iz-VO-lee-teh	Go ahead; You first
Požurite	po-zhoo-REE-teh	Hurry up
Kao to	kow toh	Like that
Evo	EH-vo	Here it is

An expression of affection:

Ja te volim	ya teh VO-lim	I like you very much

And otherwise:

Izgubi se!	iz-GOOB-ee seh	Get lost!

Polish

Polish	Po polsku	po-POHL-skoo

SEE THE PRONUNCIATION GUIDE ON PAGE 159.

Good day	Dzień dobry	dzhen DOH-brih
Good evening	Dobry wieczór	DOH-brih VYEH-chur
How are you?	Jak się pan miewa? (m) Jak się pani miewa? (f)	yahk sheh pahn MYEH-va yahk sheh PA-nee MYEH-va
Very well	Bardzo dobrze	BAR-dzo DOHB-zheh
Happy to meet you	Bardzo mi miło	BAR-dzo mee MEE-woh
Good-bye	Do widzenia	doh veed-ZEHN-ya
My name	Moje nazwisko	MO-yeh nah-ZVEE-sko

Your name	Pana nazwisko	PA-na nah-ZVEE-sko
Mrs. (and) Mr.	Pani (i) Pan	PA-nee (ee) pahn
Miss	Panna	PAHN-na
Yes	Tak	tahk
No; not	Nie	nyeh
Excuse me	Przepraszam pana	psheh-PRA-shahm PA-na
Please	Proszę	PRO-sheh
Thank you	Dziękuję	djen-KOO-yeh
You're welcome	Proszę bardzo	PRO-sheh BAR-dzo
Again	Znowu	ZNOH-voo
Wait	Czekać	CHEH-kahch
Enough	Dosyć	DOH-sitch
Where is	Gdzie jest	gdzheh yest
the telephone	telefon	teh-LEH-fohn
the toilet	toaleta	toh-ah-LEH-tah
the airport	lotnisko	loht-NEES-ko

the train station	stacja kolejowa	STAH-tsya ko-leh-YO-va
a bicycle	rower	RO-ver
my baggage	mój bagaż	MOO-y BAH-gahzh
the train for ___	pociąg do ___	PO-chong doh ___
the bus for ___	autobus do ___	ow-TOH-Booss doh ___
the boat for ___	okręt do ___	OHK-rent doh ___
What time?	O której godzinie?	oh KTOO-ray go-JEE-nyeh
Now; Not now	Teraz; nie teraz	TEH-rahz; nyeh TEH-rahz
Later	Później	POOZH-nyay
A bank	Bank	bahnk
A drugstore	Apteka	ahp-TEH-ka
A taxi stand	Taksówka	tahk-SOOF-ka
A market	Targ	tark
A department store	Dom Towarowy	Dohm toh-va-RO-vee

Far; not far	Daleko; nie daleko	da-LEH-ko; nyeh da-LEH-ko
Left; right	Lewo; pravo	LEH-vo; PRA-vo
Here; there	Tu; tam	too tahm
Open; closed	Otwarte; zamknięte	oht-var-TEH; zahm-K'NYEN-teh
Beautiful	Piękne	P'YENK-neh
How much?	Ile?	EE-leh
Very expensive	Bardzo drogi	BAR-dzo DRO-ghee
Less expensive	Nie tak drogi	n'yeh tahk DRO-ghee
Another color	Inny kolor	EE-ne-nee KOH-lor
Larger	Większy	VYENK-shee
Smaller	Mniejszy	MNYAY-shee
Hotel	Hotel	HO-tel
A room (and bath)	Pokój (z łazienka)	po-KOO-ee (zh wa-ZHEN-koh)
Today	Dzisiaj	DZHEE-shy
Tomorrow	Jutro	YOOT-ro

___ days*	___ dni	___ d'nee
What number?	Jaki numer?	YAH-kee NOO-mer
Good; not good	Dobry; niedobry	DOH-bree; nyeh-DOH-bree
A restaurant	Restauracja	ress-toh-RA-ts'ya
Soup	Zupa	ZOO-pa
Meat	Mięso	m'YEN-so
Chicken	Kura	KOO-ra
Fish	Ryba	RIH-ba
Omelet	Omlet	OHM-let
Vegetables	Jarzyny	yah-ZHEE-nee
Potatoes	Ziemniaki	zhem-NYA-kee
Bread	Chleb	hlep
Mineral water	Woda mineralna	VO-da mee-neh-RAHL-na
Wine (or) beer	Wino (lub) piwo	VEE-no (loop) PEE-vo
Coffee; tea	Kawa; herbata	KA-va; hair-BA-ta

*For numbers see page 155.

Milk	Mleko	MLEH-ko
Dessert	Deser	DEH-sehr
Delicious	Smaczne	SMAHCH-neh
Police	Policja	po-LEE-t'syah
Doctor	Doktór	DOK-toor
Dentist	Dentysta	den-TISS-ta
Sick	Chory	KHO-ree
Pain	Ból	bool
Do you understand?	Rozumiesz?	ro-ZOO-myesh
I don't understand	Nie rozumiem	nyem ro-ZOO-myem
Slowly	Powoli	po-VO-lee
Possible	Możliwe	mohzh-LEE-veh
What is this?	Co to jest?	tso toh yest

NUMBERS

0	zero	ZEH-ro
1	jeden	YEH-den
2	dwa	dva
3	trzy	tr'zhee

4	cztery	CH'TEH-ree
5	pięć	pyench
6	sześć	shesht
7	siedem	SHYEH-dem
8	osiem	OH-sh'yem
9	dziewięć	JEV-yench
10	dziesięć	JESH-yench
11	jedennaście	yeh-den-NAHSH-cheh
12	dwanaście	dva-NAHSH-cheh
13	trzynaście	trzh-NAHSH-cheh
14	czternaście	ch'tehr-NAHSH-cheh
15	piętnaście	p'yent-NAHSH-cheh
16	szesnaście	shes-NAHSH-cheh
17	siedemnaście	shyeh-dem-NAHSH-cheh
18	osiemnaście	o-shem-NAHSH-cheh
19	dziewiętnaście	jeh-vent-NAHSH-cheh

20	dwadzieścia	dva-JESH-cha
21 (etc.)	dwadzieścia jeden	dva-JESH-cha YEH-den
30	trzydzieści	tshee-JESH-chee
40	czterdzieści	ch'tehr-JESH-chee
50	pięćdziesiąt	pyench-JESH-ownt
60	sześćdziesiąt	sheht-JESH-ownt
70	siedemdziesiąt	shyeh-dem-JESH-ownt
80	osiemdziesiąt	o-shem-JESH-ownt
90	dziewięćdziesiąt	jeh-vyench-JESH-shownt
100	sto	sto
1,000	tysiąc	TIH-shownts
100,000	stotysięcy	sto TIH-shown-tsee
1,000,000	milion	MEE-lyohn

For Telling Time

To state the time and make appointments, add the word for "hour," *godzina* (go-JEE-na) to the number. Hours are indicated by ordinal numbers—"first," "second," "third," and so on, *not* by cardinal numbers.

What time is it?	Która godzina jest?	KTOO-ra go-JEE-na yest
Two o'clock (the second hour)	Druga godzina	droo-GA go-JEE-na
Half past two (halfway to three)	W poł do trzeciej	f poo doh t'shet-yeh
Three o'clock (the third hour)	Trzecia godzina	TSHT-ya go-JEE-na
Five minutes to one	Pierwsza za pięć minity	P'YERV-sha za p'yench mee-NEE-tee

POLISH

Polish, a Slavic language, is quite close to Russian and the other Slavic languages. Since Poland has been a battleground for centuries, suffering invasions from various countries, it has, as might be expected, undergone some linguistic changes. A "friendly" invasion by Napoleon, who seemed almost a liberator to the Poles, has left an interest in French language and culture, reciprocated by the French admiration for Polish culture.

The use of the Roman instead of the Cyrillic
alphabet by the Poles was an important point of
separation from the Eastern Slavs, the Russians.
This choice of alphabet stems from the early con-
version of the Polish people to Roman Catholicism; the Russians were converted to the Eastern
branch of Christianity by missionaries from Constantinople. Roman Catholicism has recently been
highlighted in Poland by the ascension of Pope
John Paul II, the first Polish prelate in history to
become pope. The influence of Latin, the language
of the Catholic Church, has been another active
element in keeping Poland associated with Western Europe.

Although Polish is written in the Roman alphabet, there are many marks and spelling combinations that may seem odd to English-speakers. See
the list below for some of the principal modifica-
tions necessary to pronounce words in Polish.

ą = own (nasalized)

c = ts

ć = ch

cj = tsy', with the *y* as in "yellow"
    (cja = tsya, etc.)

ćw = chv

dź = j

ę = en (nasalized)

j = y as in "yellow"

ł = w

ś, sz = sh

szcz = sh'ch

w = v

ż, ź = zh

The name of the Solidarity trade union leader Lech Wałęsa, has been mispronounced for years by Western news commentators; they fail to note that *w* is pronounced like "v," that slashed *l (ł)* is pronounced "w," that *ę* is pronounced "en" (nasalized): *Wałęsa,* then, is pronounced "Vawensa." Words of Latin origin differ somewhat from their English counterparts: *solidarność, ewolucja,* and *rewolucja* are hard to recognize as "solidarity," "evolution," and "revolution."

SOME COMMON EXPRESSIONS

Czy Pan mówi po polsku? (m)	chee pahn MOO-vee po POHL-skoo	Do you speak Polish?
Czy Pani mówi po polsku? (f)	chee PA-nee MOO-vee po POHL-skoo	Do you speak Polish?
Czy Pan jest Amerykan inem? (m)	chee pahn yest ah-meh-ree-kah-NEE-nem	Are you American?

Czy Pani jest Amerykanką? (f)	chee PA-nee yest ah-meh-ree-KAHN-kon	Are you American?
Czym mogę służyc?	chim MO-gen SWOO-zheech	May I help you?
Która jest godzina?	K'TOO-ra yest go-DZHEE-na	What time is it?
Nie ma za co	nyeh ma za tso	Don't mention it
Na zdrowie!	na ZDRO-vee-yeh	To your health!
Prędko	PREND-ko	Hurry

And in a romantic mood:

Piękna	P'YEN-k'na	Beautiful
Przystojny	pshee-STOY-nee	Handsome
Kocham cię	KO-hahm chyeh	I love you

And otherwise:

Głupiec	GWOO-p'yets	Fool
Idiota	eed-YO-ta	Idiot

Hungarian

Hungarian	Magyarul	MAW-jar-ool

SEE THE PRONUNCIATION GUIDE ON PAGE 170.

Good day	Jó napot	yo NAW-pot
Good evening	Jó estét	yo ESH-tate
How are you?	Hogy van?	hodj vawn
Very well	Jól vagyok	yol VA-d'yok
Happy to meet you	Örvendek	UHR-ven-dek
Good-bye	Visontlátásra	VEE-sont-LA-tash-ra
My name	A nevem	aw NEH-vem
Your name	A neve	aw NEH-veh
Mr. (and) Mrs.	Úr (és) Né (after name)	oor (aysh) nay
Miss	Kisasszony (after name)	KISH-aw-sohn'
Yes	Igen	EE-ghen
No; not	Nem	nem

Excuse me	Bocsásson meg	BO-cha-shon mehg
Please	Kérem	KAY-rem
Thank you	Köszönöm	KUH-suh-num
You're welcome	Kérem	KAY-rem
Again	Ismét	EESH-meht
Wait	Várjon	VAR-yon
Enough	Elég	EH-layg
Where is	Hol van	hohl vawn
the telephone	telephon	TEH-leh-fon
the toilet	klozet	KLO-zet
the airport	a repülö tër	aw REH-pew-luh tehr
the train station	az állomás	awz AH-lo-mahsh
a bicycle	bicikli	BEE-tsee-klee
my baggage	a böröndöm	aw BUH-ruhn-duhm
the train for ___	a vonat ___ nok	aw VO-naht ___ nock

the bus for ___	az autobusz ___ nok	awz OW-toh-boos ___ nock
the boat for ___	a hajó ___ nok	aw HAW-yo ___ nock
What time?	Hány órakkor?	hahn O-ra-kohr
Now; not now	Most; nem most	mosht; nem mosht
Later	Késöbb	KAY-shuhb
A bank	A bank	aw bawnk
A drugstore	A patika	aw PAW-tee-kaw
A taxi	A taxi	aw TAHK-see
A market	A piac	aw PEE-awts
A department store	Az árúház	awz AH-roo-hahz
Far; not far	Messze; nem messze	MES-seh; nem MES-seh
Left; right	Bal; job	bawl; yob
Here; there	Itt; ott	it; oht
Open; closed	Nyitva; zarva	NYEET-vaw; ZAHR-vaw
Beautiful	Szép	sayp

How much?	Mennyi?	MEHN-nyee
Very expensive	Nagyon drága	NAWD-yohn DRA-gaw
Less expensive	Olcsóbb	ALL-chob
Another color	Más szinü	mahsh SEE-new
Larger	Nagyobb	NAWD-yob
Smaller	Kisebb	KEY-sheb
Hotel	Szálloda	SA-lo-daw
A room (with bath)	A szoba (fürdő vel)	aw SO-baw (FEWR-dew vel)
Today	Ma	maw
Tomorrow	Holnap	HOHL-nawp
___ days*	___ napok	___ NAW-pock
What number?	Milyen szám?	MEE-yen sahm
Good; not good	Jó; nem jó	yo; nem yo
A restaurant	A vendéglő	aw VEN-deh-gluh
Soup	Leves	LEH-vesh

*For numbers see page 167.

Meat	Hús	hoosh
Chicken	Csirke	CHEER-keh
Fish	Hal	hawl
Eggs	Tojás	TOH-yahsh
Vegetables	Fözelék	FUH-zeh-lehk
Potatoes	Krumpli	KROOM-plee
Bread	Kenyér	KEN-yehr
Mineral water	Ásványvíz	AHSH-vahn'-veez
Wine (or) beer	Bor (vagy) sör	bor (voj) shuhrr
Coffee; tea	Kávé; tea	KA-vay; TEH-aw
Milk	Tej	tay
Dessert	Csemege	CHEH-meh-geh
Delicious	Kitünö	KEE-tew-nuh
Police	Rendörség	REN-duhr-sheg
Doctor	Orvos	OR-vosh
Dentist	Fog orvos	fog OR-vosh
Sick	Beteg	BEH-teg
Pain	Fáidalom	FIE-daw-lom

Do you understand?	Erti?	AIR-tee
I don't understand	Nem ertem	nem AIR-tem
Slowly	Lassan	LAWSH-shawn
Possible	Lehetséges	LEH-het-shay-ghesh
What is this?	Mi ez?	mee ez

NUMBERS

0	nulla	NOO-la
1	egy	edj
2	kettő	KÉT-tuh
3	három	HA-rohm
4	négy	nedj
5	öt	uht
6	hat	hawt
7	hét	heht
8	nyolc	n'yohlts
9	kilenc	KEE-lents
10	tíz	teez

11	tizenegy	TEE-zen-edj
12	tizenkettő	TEE-zen-ket-tuh
13	tizenhárom	TEE-zen-ha-rohm
14	tizennégy	TEE-zen-nedj
15	tizenöt	TEE-zen-uht
16	tizenhat	TEE-zen-haht
17	tizenhét	TEE-zen-nate
18	tizennyolc	TEE-zen-n'yohlts
19	tizenkilenc	TEE-zen-kee-lents
20	húsz	hooss
21 (etc.)	húszonégy	HOOSS-oh-nedj
30	harminc	HAR-mintz
40	negyven	NEDJ-ven
50	ötven	UHT-ven
60	hatvan	HAHT-von
70	hetven	HET-ven
80	nyolcvan	N'YOHLTS-von

90	kilencven	KEE-lents-ven
100	száz	sahz
1,000	ezer	EH-zer
100,000	százezer	SAHZ-eh-zer
1,000,000	millió	MEEL-yo

For Telling Time

What time is it?	Hány óra van?	hahnh OH-raw vawn
It's six o'clock	Hat óra van	hawt OH-raw vawn
It's three o'clock	Három óra van	HA-rom OH-raw vawn
Ten past two	Tíz percel múlt kettő	teez PEHRT-zel moolt KET-tuh
Two thirty	Fél három	fail HA-rom (halfway to three)

HUNGARIAN

Hungarian differs from the languages of most other European nations, which share a major language group (Romance, Slav, or Germanic) with neighboring countries. There are no countries surrounding Hungary that have a language similar to Hungarian. Languages in countries some distance away are related—Finnish, Estonian, and Turkish, for example—but not mutually understandable to native speakers the way Spanish and Italian are. To find a language somewhat closer to Hungarian, one would have to journey far into Siberia and find the remnants of the Modvin and Chermiss peoples, far off in time and distance but linguistically close to Hungarian.

Hungarian descended not from Latin but from the language of the Huns, that great wave of horsemen who swept into Europe from Asia in ancient times and seriously threatened the Roman Empire. They might have successfully toppled the empire had it not been for the death of their supreme leader, Attila, whose name is still associated with destruction, except in Hungary. There, Attila is still a favored name for boys.

Hungarian enjoys a simple grammar as far as verbs and noun gender are concerned, but its vocal combinations are difficult to pronounce unless you have the key. Accentuation of words is easy: they are all stressed on the first syllable.

Note the value of certain letters or letter combinations in Hungarian:

a = aw
á = ah
c = ts
cs = ch
é = eh or ay

j = y as in "yellow"
ó = oh
ő = long o
ö = uh
s = sh
sz = s
ú = oo
ű = long u
ü = ew

SOME COMMON EXPRESSIONS

Beszél magyarul?	BEH-sail MAW-jar-ool	Do you speak Hungarian?
Maga amerikai?	MA-ga AH-meh-ree-ka-ee	Are you American?
Maga angol?	MA-ga AHN-gohl	Are you English?
Isten hozta	ISH-ten HOHZ-ta	Welcome
Egészségére!	EH-gay-sheh-geh-reh	To your health!
Mi történt?	mee TUHR-tehnt	What happened?
Tilos	TEE-losh	Forbidden
Miért nem?	MEE-ehrt nem	Why not?

| Beleegyezem | BEH-leh-eh-g'yehz-ehm | Agreed ("I agree") |
| Viszontlátásra | VEE-sont-la-tash-ra | See you again. |

And on a romantic note:

| Drágám | DRA-gahm | My dear |
| Angyalom | AHN-ja-lom | My angel |

Or less friendly terms:

| Ügyetlen | EW-jet-len | clumsy |
| Boland | BO-land | Crazy |

Romanian

Romanian	Româneşte	ro-muh-NESH-teh

NOTE: Because of the Latin connection, Romanian words are fairly easy to pronounce. If you visit this pleasant country, which is now encouraging tourism, keep in mind the following: *ă* and *â* are pronounced "uh"; *c* before *e* or *i,* "ch"; *g* before *e* or *i,* "j"; *ş* is pronounced "sh"; and *ţ* is pronounced "ts."

Good day	Bună ziua	BOO-nuh ZEE-wa
Good evening	Bună seara	BOO-nuh seh-AH-ra
How are you?	Ce mai faceţi?	cheh my FA-chets'
Very well	Foarte bine	fo-AR-teh BEE-neh
Happy to meet you	Încîntat	uhn-kuhn-TAHT
Good-bye	La revedere	la reh-veh-DEH-reh

My name	Numele meu	NOO-meh-leh MEH-oo
Your name	Cum vă numiţi	koom vuh noo-MEETS
Mr. (and) Mrs.	Domnul (şi) Doamna	DOHM-nool (shee) do-AHM-na
Miss	Domnişoară	DOHM-nee-shoo-AH-ruh
Yes	Da	da
No; not	Nu	noo
Excuse me	Scuzăţi-mi	skoo-ZA-tsee-muh
Please	Vă rog	vuh-ROHG
Thank you	Mulţumesc	mool-tsoo-MESK
You're welcome	Bine aţi venit	BEE-neh atsi veh-NEET
Again	Iarăşi	YA-ruhsh'
Wait	Aşteptaţi	ahsh-tep-TAHTS'
Enough	Destul	deh-STOOL
Where is	Unde este	OON-deh YES-teh
the telephone	telefonul	teh-leh-FOHN-ool

the toilet	toaleta	twah-LEH-ta
the airport	aeroportul	ah-eh-ro-PORT-ool
the train station	gara	GA-ra
a bicycle	bicicleta	bee-chee-CLEH-ta
my baggage	bagajul meu	ba-GAH-zhool MEH-oo
the train for ___	trenul pentru ___	trehn-OOL PEN-troo ___
the bus for ___	autobusul pentru ___	ow-toh-BOOS-ool PEN-troo ___
the boat for ___	vaporul pentru ___	va-PO-rool PEN-troo ___
What time?	Lace oră?	la-CHEH OH-ruh
Now; not now	Acum; nu acum	ah-KOOM; noo ah-KOOM
Later	Mai tîrziu	my tuhr-Z'YOO

A bank	Bancă	BAHN-kuh
A drugstore	Farmacie	far-ma-CHEE-eh
A taxi	Taxi	ta-K'SEE
A market	Piaţă	P'YA-tsuh
A department store	Magazinul universal	ma-ga-ZEE-nool oo-nee-ver-SAHL
Far; not far	Departe; nu departe	deh-PAR-teh; noo deh-PAR-teh
Left; right	Stînga; dreapta	STUHN-ga; dreh-AP-ta
Here; there	Aici; acolo	ah-EECH'; ah-KO-lo
Open; closed	Deschis; închis	des-KEES; uhn-KEES
Beautiful	Frumos (m) Frumoasă (f)	froo-MOHS froo-mo-AH-suh
How much?	Cît costă?	kuht KO-stuh
Very expensive	Foarte scump	fo-AHR-teh scoomp
Less expensive	Mai ieftin	my YEF-teen

Another color	Altă culoare	AL-tuh koo-lo-AH-reh
Larger	Mai mare	my MA-reh
Smaller	Mai mic	my meek
Hotel	Hotel	(pronounced as in English)
A room (with bath)	Cameră (cu baie)	KA-meh-ruh (koo BA-yeh)
Today	Astăzi	ah-STUZ'
Tomorrow	Mîine	MUH-ee-neh
____ days*	____ zile	____ ZEE-leh
What number?	Ce număr?	cheh NOO-muhr
Good; not good	Bun; no bun	boon; noo boon
Restaurant	Restaurant	reh-stah-oo-RAHNT
Soup	Supă	SOO-puh
Meat	Carne	KAR-neh
Chicken	Pui	POO'ee
Fish	Peşte	PESH-teh
Eggs	Ouă	O-wuh

*For numbers see page 179.

Vegetables	Legume	leh-GOOM-eh
Potatoes; rice	cartofi; orez	kar-TOFF'; oh-REZ
Bread	Pîine	puh-EE-neh
Mineral water	Apă minerală	AH-puh mee-neh-RA-luh
Wine; beer	Vin; bere	veen; BEH-reh
Coffee; tea	Cafea; ceai	Ka-FEH-ah; chay
Milk	Lapte	LAHP-teh
Dessert	Desert	deh-SERT
Delicious	Delicios	deh-leech-YOHS
Police	Miliţie	mee-LEET-see-yeh
Doctor	Doctor	DOK-tor
Dentist	Dentist	den-TEEST
Sick	Bolnav	bol-NAHV
Pain	Durere	dooh-REH-reh
Do you understand?	Înţelegeţi?	uhn-tse-LEH-d'jets
I don't understand	Nu înţeleg	noo uhn-t'sel-LEG
Slowly	Încet	uhn-CHET

Possible	Posibil	poh-SEE-beel
What is this?	Ce este asta?	cheh YESS- teh AHSS-ta

NUMBERS

0	zero	ZEH-ro
1	unu	OO-noo
2	doi	doy
3	trei	trey
4	patru	PA-troo
5	cinci	chinch'
6	şase	SHA-seh
7	şapte	SHA-p'teh
8	opt	opt
9	nouă	NO-wuh
10	zece	ZEH-cheh
11	unsprezece	OON-spreh- ZEH-cheh
12	doisprezece	DOY-spreh- ZEH-cheh
13	treisprezece	TREY-spreh- ZEH-cheh

14	patrusprezece	PA-troo-spreh-ZEH-cheh
15	cincisprezece	CHINCH-spreh-ZEH-cheh
16	şaisprezece	SHAY-spreh-ZEH-cheh
17	şaptesprezece	SHAHP-teh-spreh-ZEH-cheh
18	optsprezece	OPT-spreh-ZEH-cheh
19	nouăsprezece	NO-wuh-spreh-ZEH-cheh
20	douăzeci	DO-wuh-ZEHCH'
21 (etc.)	douăzecişiunu	DO-wuh-ZEHCH'-shee-oo-noo
30	treizeci	trey-ZEHCH'
40	patruzeci	pa-troo-ZEHCH'
50	cincizeci	chinch'-ZEHCH'

60	şaizeci	say-ZEHCH'
70	şaptezeci	shahp-teh-ZEHCH'
80	optzeci	opt-ZEHCH'
90	nouăzeci	noh-wuh-ZEHCH'
100	o sută	oh SOO-tuh
1,000	o mie	oh MEE-yeh
100,000	o sută demii	oh SOO-tuh de-MEE
1,000,000	un milion	oon meel-YOHN

For Telling Time

What time is it?	Cît este ceasul?	kuht YESS-teh CHA-sool
It's two o'clock	Este ora două	YESS-teh O-ra DOH-wuh
It's ten past two	Este ora două şi zece	YESS-teh O-ra DOH-wuh shee ZEH-cheh
Half past two	Ora două şi jumătate	O-ra DOH-wuh shee zhoo-muh-TA-teh

| It's ten to three | Ora trei fără zece | O-ra trey FUH-ruh ZEH-cheh |

ROMANIAN

The words *Romania* and *Romanian* are derived from *Roma,* the Latin name of the capital of the Roman Empire. The empire's linguistic boundaries were represented by Portuguese in the west and Romanian in the east, and both these Romance languages retain entire words, spellings, and other features of Latin.

Romania, originally called Dacia, was chosen as a retirement site for veterans of the Roman legions, and these veterans kept Latin alive in the area, although the Roman language slowly changed as words from other tongues began to infiltrate over time.

A large part of modern Romania is called Transylvania; the legendary home of Dracula is a region that has passed back and forth between Turkey, Hungary, and Romania for generations. Dracula, as we know him today, is the creation of author Bram Stoker (his novel *Dracula* was published in 1897), but Stoker's fictional character was based on a real person. Vlad Dracul was a Romanian prince who lived in the early fifteenth century. While he was not a gentle soul—*dracul* can be translated as "devil"—it is actually his son, Prince Vlad III, who was the basis for Stoker's novel.

Vlad III, or Vlad the Impaler, was a warlord
infamous for his bloody tortures of his enemies,
whether they were invading Turkish armies or
local tax dodgers. Though he is remembered in
Romanian history as a courageous freedom fighter,
he can't seem to shake his reputation as a vampire.
An interesting contemporary note: one of his direct
descendants was located several years ago in a Bu-
charest hospital, where he was working in a blood
bank!

SOME COMMON EXPRESSIONS

Vorbiţi româneşte?	vor-BEETS' ro-muh-NESH-teh	Do you speak Romanian?
Sînteţi american? (m)	suhn-TETS' ah-meh-ree-KAHN	Are you American?
Sînteţi americană? (f)	suhn-TETS' ah-meh-ree-KA-nuh	Are you American?
Sînteţi englez? (m)	suhn-TETS' en-GLEHZ	Are you English?
Sînteţi ? englezoaică (f)	suhn-TETS' en-gleh-ZWAY-kuh	Are you English?
Intraţi	EEN-TRAHTS'	Come in.

Vă rog	vuh rog	After you; Please
Grăbiţi-vă	gruh-BEETS'-vuh	Hurry up
Hai noroc!	hai no-ROK	To your health! (when drinking)
Sănătate	suh-nuh-TA-teh	To your health; Bless you (after someone sneezes)
Ce doriţi?	cheh doh-REETS'	What do you wish?
Drum bun	droom BOON	A pleasant journey

And on a friendly note:

Sînteţi amabil	suhn-TETS' ah-ma-BEEL	Would you please
Te iubesc	teh yoo-BESK	I love you

And otherwise:

Tîmpitule	tuhm-PEET-oo-leh	Stupid one

Greek

Greek	Ἑλληνικὰ	Eh-lee-nee-KA
Good day	Καλημέρα	ka-lee-MEH-ra
Good evening	Καλησπέρα	ka-lee-SPE-ra
How are you?	Πῶς εἶσθε;*	pohs EES-theh
Very well	Πολὺ καλὰ	po-LEE ka-LA
Happy to meet you	Χαίρω πολὺ	HEH-ro po-LEE
Good bye	Ἀντίο	ah-DEE-oh
My name	Τὸ ὄνομά μου	toh HO-no-MA moo
Your name	Τὸ ὄνομά σας	toh HO-no-MA sas
Mr. (and) Mrs.	Κύριος (καὶ) Κυρία	KEE-ree-os (ke) kee-REE-ya
Miss	Δεσποινὶς	thess-peh-NEESS
Yes	Ναὶ	nay
No/not	Ὄχι/δὲν	OH-hee/then

*A semicolon in Greek is equivalent to our question mark.

Excuse me	Μὲ συγχωρεῖτε	meh seen-ho-REE-teh
Please	Παρακαλῶ	pa-ra-ka-LO
Thank you	Εὐχαριστῶ	ef-ha-ree-STO
You're welcome	Τίποτα	TEE-po-ta
Again	Πάλι	PA-lee
Wait	Περίμενε	peh-REE-meh-neh
Enough	Ἀρχετὰ	ar-ke-TA
Where is	Ποῦ εἶναι	pou EE-nay
the telephone	Τὸ τηλέφωνο	toh tee-LEH-fo-no
the toilet	Τὸ ἀποχωρη-τήριο	toh ah-po-ho-ree-TEE-ree-yo
the airport	ὁ ἀερο-λιμὴν	oh ah-eh-ro-lee-MEEN
the train station	ὁ σταθμὸς τοῦ τραίνου	oh stath-MOHSS too TREH-noo
the subway	ὁ ὑπόγειος	oh hi-PO-ghee-os
my baggage	οἱ ἀποσκευές μου	hi a-po-skeh-VES moo
the train for _____	Τὸ τραῖνο γιὰ _____	toh TREH-no ya _____

the bus for ___	τὸ λεωφορεῖο γιὰ ___	to leh-oh-fo-REE-o ya ___
the boat for ___	τὸ πλοῖο γιὰ ___	toh PLEE-yo ya ___
What time?	Τί ὥρα;	tee OH-ra
Now	Τώρα	TOH-ra
Not now	ὄχι τώρα	OH-hee TOH-ra
Later	Ἀργότερα	ar-GO-teh-ra
A bank	Μιὰ τράπεζα	MEE-ya TRA-peh-za
A drugstore	Ἔνα φαρμακεῖο	EH-na far-ma-KEE-yo
A taxi stand	Ἔνας σταθμὸς ταξὶ	EH-nas stath-MOS tahk-see
A market	Μιὰ ἀγορὰ	MEE-ya a-go-RA
A department store	Κατάστημα	ka-TA-stee-ma
Far	Μακρυὰ	ma-kree-YA
Not far	Ὄχι μακρυὰ	OH-hee ma-kree-YA
Left	Ἀριστερὰ	ah-ris-teh-RA
Right	Δεξιὰ	thek-see-YA
Here	Ἐδῶ	eh-THO

There	Ἐκεῖ	eh-KEE
Open	Ἀνοιχτὸ	a-neek-TOH
Closed	Κλειστὸ	klee-STO
Beautiful	Ὄμορφη Ὄμορφος	OH-mor-fee OH-mor-fohss
How much?	Πόσο;	PO-so
Very expensive	Πολὺ ἀκριβὸ	po-LEE ah-kree-VO
Less expensive	Φτηνότερο	f'thee-NO- teh-ro
Another color	Ἄλλο χρῶμα	ah-LO HRO-ma
Larger	Πιὸ μεγάλο	p'yo meh-GA-lo
Smaller	Πιὸ μικρὸ	p'yo mee-KRO
Hotel	Ξενοδοχεῖο	kse-no- tho-HEE-yo
A room (with bath)	Ἕνα δωμάτιο μὲ λουτρὸ	EH-na tho-MA- tee-yo-meh loo-TRO
Today	Σήμερα	SEE-meh-ra
Tomorrow	Αὔριο	AHV-ree-yo
_____ days*	_____ ἡμέρες	_____ hee- MEH-res

What number?	Τί νούμερο;	tee NOO-meh-ro
Good	Καλὸ	ka-LO
Not good	Ὄχι καλὸ	OH-hee ka-LO
A restaurant	Ἔνα ἐστιατόριο	EH-na ess-tee-ah-TOH-ree-o
Soup	Σούπα	SOO-pa
Meat	Κρέας	KREH-ahs
Chicken	Κοτόπουλο	ko-toh-POO-lo
Fish	Ψάρι	PSA-ree
Omelet	Ὀμελέτα	oh-meh-LEH-ta
Vegetables	Λαχανικὰ	la-ha-nee-KA
Potatoes	Πατάτες	pa-TA-tess
Bread	Ψωμὶ	pso-MEE
Mineral water	Μεταλλικὸ νερὸ	meh-ta-li-KO ne-RO
Wine (or) beer	Κρασὶ (ἤ) μπυρα	kra-SEE (ee) BEE-ra
Coffee (or) tea	Καφὲς (ἤ) τσάϊ	ka-FEHSS (ee) TSA-ee
Milk	Γάλα	GA-la

*For numbers see page 190.

Dessert	Ἐπιδόρπιο	heh-pee-THOR-pee-yo
Delicious	Νόστιμο	NO-stee-mo
Police	Ἀστυνομία	ahs-tee-no-MEE-ya
Doctor	Γιατρός	ya-TROS
Dentist	Ὀδοντο-γιατρός	oh-thon-doh-ya-TROHS
Sick	Ἄρρωστος	HA-ro-stohss
Pain	Πόνος	PO-nohs
Do you understand?	Καταλαβαί-νεις;	ka-ta-la-VEH-niss
I don't understand	Δὲν καταλαβαίνω	then ka-ta-la-VEH-no
Slowly	Σιγά-σιγά	see-GA, see-GA
Possible	Δυνατόν	thee-na-TON
What is this?	Τί εἶναι αὐτό;	tee ee-neh af-TOH

NUMBERS

0	mee-THEN
1	EH-nah
2	THEE-oh

3	TREE-ah
4	TEH-seh-ra
5	PEN-deh
6	EHK-see
7	ehp-TA
8	ohk-TOH
9	eh-NEH-ah
10	THEH-ka
11	EN-theh-ka
12	THO-theh-ka
13	theh-ka-TREE-ah
14	theh-ka-TEH-seh-ra
15	theh-ka-PEN-deh
16	theh-ka-EHK-see
17	theh-ka-ehp-TA
18	theh-ka-ohk-TOH
19	theh-ka-eh-NEH-ah
20	EE-ko-see
21 (etc.)	ee-ko-see-EH-na
30	tree-AHN-da
40	sa-RAHN-da

50	peh-NEEN-da
60	ehK-SEEN-da
70	ehv-doh-MEEN-da
80	ohg-DOHN-da
90	eh-neh-NEEN-da
100	eh-ka-TOH
1,000	HEEL-ya
100,000	eh-ka-TOH heel-YA-thess
1,000,000	EH-na eh-ka-TOH MEER-yo

For Telling Time

What time is it?	tee O-ra EE-nay
It's eight o'clock	EE-neh ohk-TOH O-ra
Half past eight	ohk-TOH mee-SEE
Five to nine	PEN-deh pa-RA eh-NAY-ah
At one o'clock	stahss MEE-ya *O-ra

*The word "one" (eh-NAH) has a feminine form (MEE-ya), which is used for "one o'clock" since the word for "hour" is feminine.

GREEK

Greek is one of the oldest languages of the Western world, and unlike Latin, it is still very much alive. It is spoken in modern form by millions of people in continental Greece, the Aegean islands, and throughout the Mediterranean area, as well as in the big cities of North America.

The declining Roman Empire split into western and eastern sections in the fifth century A.D. The eastern part, Byzantium, had its capital at Constantinople. The imperial power eventually passed on to the Greeks and lasted for another thousand years, until the Turks conquered Constantinople in 1453 A.D.

While more than a million Greeks used to live in Turkey, most of them were forced out after World War I. But even today the Turkish capital of Istanbul is still, to Greeks, Constantinople, the "second Rome." The name Istanbul is not a Turkish word but a rendition of the Greek expression for a "city within the walls" (*istan-polis*). The huge walls referred to are still standing.

Many other European languages start the negative with *n,* but in Greek, ναί (neh) is "yes." And certain other everyday words may surprise you. To call for a restaurant check, you ask for the λογαριασμός (lo-ga-ri-as-MOS), which brings to mind our mathematical logarithm—and is sometimes equally hard to understand.

GREEK WORDS YOU ALREADY KNOW

Visitors to Greece or those who wish to communicate with Greek-speaking people will find that they already possess a large vocabulary of Greek words. The fact that many medical, technical, and scientific words in English are of Greek origin is evidence of the long-lasting influence of Greek thought and research in Europe and the Near East. Consider, for example, the following words and their component meanings:

geography	*geo* (earth) + *graphia* (writing)
psychiatrist	*psyche* (soul) + *iatros* (doctor)
symphony	*syn* (together) + *phonia* (sound)
democracy	*demos* (people) + *kratia* (rule, power)
economy	*oikos* (house) + *nomia* (administration)
telegram	*tele* (far) + *gramma* (letter, writing)
telephone	*tele* (far) + *phonia* (sound)
plutocracy	*Pluto* (god of wealth and the underworld) + *kratia* (rule, power)
hydrophobia	*hydor* (water) + *phobia* (fear)

cardiology	*kardia* (heart) + *logos* (speech, word)
agoraphobia	*agora* (marketplace) + *phobia* (fear)
pediatrics	*pedi* (child) + *iatreia* (art of healing)
anatomy	*anatome* (dissection)
atom	*atomos* (what cannot be split) (But it was!)

SOME COMMON EXPRESSIONS

YA-su	Hello; Good-bye; Great! Bravo!
MEE-la-teh eh-lee-nee-KA	Do you speak Greek?
ka-LOHSS oh-REE-sa-teh	Welcome
stin-ee HEE-ya sahs	To your health!
en-DA-k'see	Okay
tee seem-VEH-nee	What's the matter?
pro-so-HEE	Look out
STA-su	Stop
meen ah-nee-see-HEE-teh	Don't worry

pa-ra-ka-LO	Please; You're welcome; Go ahead; You first
ka-LEE TEE-hee	Good luck
ka-LO ta-K'SEE-thee	Have a good trip

On a romantic note:

mu ah-reh-SEH-teh po-LEE	I like you very much
HREE-so-moo	My golden one
sahs ah-gha-PO	I love you

And otherwise:

mee meh-nohk-LEE-teh	Stop bothering me!
EK-so	Get out!

Turkish

Turkish	Türkce	TÜRK-cheh

NOTE: In Turkish, *c* is pronounced "j" and *ç* is "ch"; *ğ* is rendered as a slight pause (the half-moon sign, or breve, makes the letter silent); the undotted ı is pronounced "uh"; *j* is "zh"; *ö* is "er"; *ş* is "sh"; and *ü* is pronounced by saying "ee" with the lips pursed.

Good day	Gün aydın	Gün-AI-dun
Good evening	Iyi akşamlar	ee-YEE ahk-shahm-LAR
How are you?	Nasılsınız?	NA-suhl-SUH-nuhz
Very well	Iyiyim	ee-yee-YIM
Happy to meet you	Memnun oldum	mem-NOON ol-DOOM
Good-bye	Allaha ısmarladık (said by person leaving)	ah-la-HA us-mar-la-DUHK

	Güle, güle (said by person staying)	gü-LEH, gü-LEH
My name	Ismim	iss-MIM
Your name	Ismin	iss-MIN
Sir; Madam	Efendim	eh-FEN-dim (said before name)
Mrs.; Miss	Bayan	buy-YAHN
Yes	Evet	eh-VET
No; not	Hayır; yok *or* değil	ha-YUHR; yohk, deh-EEL
Excuse me	Affedersiniz	AH-fehr-der-si-NIZ
Please	Lütfen	LÜT-fen
Thank you	Teşekkür ederim	teh-shek-KÜR eh-deh-RIM
You're welcome	Rica ederim	ree-JA eh-deh-RIM
Again	Bir daha	beer da-HA
Wait	Bekle mek	bek-leh mek
Enough	Kafi	ka-FEE
Where is ____	____ nerede	NEH-reh-deh

the telephone	telefon	teh-leh-FOHN
the toilet	tuvalet	too-va-LET
the airport	hava alanı	ha-VA ah-la-NUH
the train station	tren istasyonu	trehn iss-sta-s'yo-NUH
the bicycle	bisiklet	bee-see-KLET
my baggage	benim bagajım	beh-NIM ba-ga-ZHUHM
the train for ___	___'e giden tren	___ eh ghi-DEN tren
the bus for ___	___'e giden otobüs	___ eh ghi-DEN oh-toh-BÜSS
the boat for ___	___'e giden vapur	___ eh ghi-DEN va-POOR
What time?	Saat kaçta?	sa-aht kahch-TA
Now; Not now	Şimdi; şimdi değil	SHIM-dee; SHIM-dee deh-EEL
Later	Daha sonra	da-HA son-RA

A bank	Banka	BAHN-ka
A drugstore	Eczane	edj-za-NEH
A taxi	Taksi	TAHK-see
A market	Çarşı	Char-SHUH
A department store	Mağaza	ma-ah-ZA
Far; not far	Uzak; uzak değil	oo-ZAHK; oo-ZAHK deh-EEL
Left; right	Sola; sağ	so-la; sah'
Here; there	Burada; orada	BOO-ra-da; OH-ra-da
Open; closed	Açık; kapalı	ah-CHUHK ka-pa-luh
Beautiful	Güzel	gü-ZEL
How much?	Kaç para?	kahch pa-RA
Very expensive	Çok pahali	chok pa-ha-LEE
Less expensive	Çok ucuz	chok oo-CHOOZ
Another color	başka renk	bahsh-KA renk
Larger	Daha büyük	da-HA bü-YÜK

Smaller	Daha küçük	da-HA kü-chük
Hotel	Otel	O-tel
A room (with bath)	(Banyolu) Oda	(BAHN-yo-loo) O-da
Today	Bugün	BOO-gün
Tomorrow	Yarın	YA-ruhn
_____ days*	_____ gün	_____ gün
What number?	Hangi numara?	HAHN-ghi, NOO-ma-ra
Good; not good	Iyi; iyi değil	ee-YEE; ee-YEE deh-EEL
A restaurant	Lokanta	lo-KAHN-ta
Soup	Çorba	chor-BA
Meat	Et	ett
Chicken	Piliç	pee-LEECH
Fish	Balık	ba-LUHK
Omelet	Omlet	ohm-LETT
Vegetables	Sebze	seb-ZEH
Rice	Pirinç	pee-RINCH
Bread	Ekmek	ek-MEK

*For numbers see page 203.

Mineral water	Şişe suyu	shee-SHEH soo-YOO
Wine (or) beer	Şarap (veya) bira	sha-RAHP (veh-YAH) BEE-ra
Coffee; tea	Kahve; çay	ka-VEH; chai
Milk	Süt	süt
Dessert	Tatlı	tut-LUH
Delicious	Lezzetli	lez-zet-LEE
Police	Polis	po-LEESS
Doctor	Doctor	dahk-TOR
Dentist	Diş tabibi	dish ta-BEE-bee
Sick	Hasta	hahss-TA
Pain	Ağrı	ah-RUH
Do you understand?	Anlıyor musun?	AHN-luh-yor moo-SOON
I don't understand	Anlamıyorum	ahn-LA-muh-YO-rum
Slowly	Yavaş	ya-VAHSH
Possible	Mümkün	müm-KÜN
What is this?	Bu nedir?	boo neh-DEER

NUMBERS

0	sifir	sih-FIHR
1	bir	beer
2	iki	ee-KEE
3	üç	üch
4	dört	dirt
5	beş	besh
6	altı	ahl-TUH
7	yedi	yeh-DEE
8	sekiz	seh-KIZ
9	dokuz	doh-KOOZ
10	on	ohn
11	on bir	ohn beer
12	on iki	ohn ee-KEE
13	on üç	ohn üch
14	on dört	ohn dirt
15	on beş	ohn besh
16	on altı	ohn AHL-tuh
17	on yedi	ohn YEH-dee
18	on sekiz	ohn SEH-kiz

19	on dokuz	ohn DOH-kooz
20	yirmi	yeer-MEE
21 (etc.)	yirmi bir	yeer-MEE beer
30	otuz	o-TOOZ
40	kırk	kirk
50	elli	el-LEE
60	altmiş	alt-MIHSH
70	yetmiş	yet-MISH
80	seksen	sek-SEHN
90	doksan	dohk-SAHN
100	yüz	yüz
1,000	bin	been
10,000	on bin	ohn been
1,000,000	milyon	meel-YOHN

For Telling Time

What time is it?	Saat kaç	SA'at katch
It's one	Saat bir	SA'at beer
It's one-thirty	Saat bir otuz	SA'at beer o-TOOZ

| It's twenty to ten | saat ona yirmi var | SA'at O-na yeer-MEE vahz |
| It's quarter past eleven | On bir çeyrek geçiyor | ohn beer CHEY-rek geh-chee-YOR |

TURKISH

It has been observed that a person who spoke only Turkish could journey from Constantinople (now Istanbul) to Peking (now Beijing) without language difficulty. At many points on his way he would pass through Turkish- or Turkic-speaking areas—the Soviet Socialist Republic of Russia, the western Chinese provinces (where the Uighur people speak a Turkic language), then northeast to Beijing, still encountering numerous tribal Turkic-speaking pockets on the way. Although Turkish power, which once dominated Eastern Europe, was stopped at the gates of Vienna in the seventeenth century, Turkish is still widely spoken in the Balkans. There is a continuous Turkic-speaking line from the Balkans to Beijing—a line as long as the trails of the Tartar and Mongol horsemen from Asia who conquered the vast territories from central Asia to eastern Europe.

Turkish, formerly written in the Arabic alphabet, is now, in the interests of modernization and simplicity, written in the Roman alphabet.

TURKISH WORDS YOU ALREADY KNOW

adres	address
doktor	*doctor*
fotograf filmi	film
hokey	hockey
kart postal	postcard
kravat	tie
manikür	manicure
masaj	massage
mesaj	message
motör	motor
müzik	music
otel	hotel
paket	package
pantalon	pants
park	parking garage
parti	party (political)
pasaport	passport
patenta	patent
sinema	cinema
soda	soda

telefon	telephone
telegraf	telegram
televizyon	television
viski	whiskey

SOME COMMON EXPRESSIONS

Selamlar	seh-lahm-LAR	Greetings
Merhaba	MEHR-ha-ba	Hello
Türkçe biliyor musumuz?	TÜRK-cheh bee-lee-YOR mu-suh-MOOZ	Do you speak Turkish?
Biraz	beer-AHZ	A little
Şerefinize!	sheh-reh-fee-neez-EH	To your health!
Dikkat!	dik-kaht	Danger! Attention!
Aferin!	AH-fer-in	Bravo!
Ne var, ne yok?	neh var, neh yohk	What's happening?
Bir şey değil	beer shey deh-EEL	It's nothing; You're welcome
Değil mi?	deh-EEL mih	Isn't it so?

İnşallah	in-SHAHL-la	If God wills
Buyurun	boo-YOO-roon	Welcome; Come in; After you
Iyi eğlenceler	ee-YEE eh-len-jeh-LEHR	Enjoy yourself
Uğurlu olsun	oo-oor-LOO ol-SOON	Good luck ("May it bring you luck")
Tebrikler	teh-brik-LEHR	Congratulations
Yok	yohk	No; There isn't any

Some words of admiration:

Ne güzel!	neh gü-ZEL	How beautiful!

And the opposite:

Köpek	ker-PEK	Dog
Ahmak	ah-MAHK	Fool

Hebrew	eh-VREET

NOTE: Hebrew is written and read from right to left. The phonetic spellings in the right column are written from left to right, as in English.

Good day	שלום	sha-LOHM
Good evening	ערב־טוב	eh-rev-Tov
How are you?	מה שלומך	ma-shlohm-KHAH (m
	מה שלומך	ma shlo-MEKH (f)
Very well	טוב מאד	tohv meh-OHD
Happy (to meet you)	נעים מאד	na-EEM lee meh-OHD
Good-bye	שלום	sha-LOHM
My name	שמי	shmee
Your name	שמך	sheem-KHAH (m)
	שמך	sh'mekh (f)
Mr.	אדון	ah-DOHN
Mrs.; Miss	גברת	GVEH-ret
Yes	כן	kehn
No; not	לא	lo
Excuse me	תסלח לי	tis-LAHKH-lee
Please	בבקשה	beh-va-ka-SHA

Thank you	תודה	toh DAH
You're welcome	על לא דבר	ahl lo-da-VAR
Again	שוב	shoov
Wait, please	נא לחכות	Na-leh-kha-KOHT
Enough	מספיק	ma-SPEEK
Where is	איפה	eh-FO
the telephone	טלפון	TEH-leh-FOHN
the toilet	בית שימוש	beht shee-MOOSH
the airport	נמל תעופה	na-MAHL teh-oo-FA
the train station	תחנת הרכבת	ta-ha-NAHT ha-ra-KEH-veht
the train	רכבת	ra-KEH-veht
my baggage	מזודה שלי	miz-va-DA she-LEE
the train for __	רכבת ל __	ra-KEH-veht leh __
the bus for __	אוטובוס ל__	OH-toh-boos leh __
the boat for __	סירה ל __	see-RA leh __
What time?	באיזו שעה	beh-EH-zoh sha-AH
Now; not now	עכשיו	ahkh-SHAHV;
	לא עכשיו	lo ahkh-SHAHV

Later	אחר כך	ah-HAR kah'kh
A bank	בנק	bahnk
A drugstore	בית מרקחת	beht-mehr-KA-haht
A taxi	מונית	mo-NEET
A market	שוק	shook
A department store	חנות־כלבו	ha-NOOT kol-BOH
Far; not far	רחוק; לא רחוק	ra-HOHK; lo -ra-'HOH
Left; right	ימינה שמאלה	SMO-la; yeh-MEE-na
Here; there	שם, פה	po; shahm
Open; closed	סגור, פתוח	pa-TOO-ahkh; sa-GOOI
Beautiful	יפה	ya-FEH (m)
	יפה	ya-FA (f)
How much?	כמה	KA-ma
Very expensive	מאד יקר	meh-OHD ya-KAR
Less expensive	פחות יקר	pa-KHOHT ya-KAR
Another color	צבע אחר	tseh-VA ah-KEHR
Larger	יותר גדול	yo-TEHR ga-DOHL
Smaller	יותר קטן	yo-TEHR ka-TAHN

Hotel	מלון	ma-LOHN
A room (with bath)	חדר עם אמבטיה	KHEH-dehr (im ahm-BAHT-ya)
Today	היום	ha-YOHM
Tomorrow	מחר	ma-HAR
— days*	ימים —	— ya-MIM
What number?	איזה מספר	eh-ZEH mees-PAR
Good; not good	טוב; לא טוב	tohv; lo tohv
A restaurant	מסעדה	miss-AH-da
Soup	מרק	MA-rah
Meat	בשר	ba-SAHR
Chicken	עף	ohf
Fish	דג	dahg
Omelet	חביטה	kha-vee-TA
Vegetables	ירקות	yeh-ra-KOHT
Potatoes	תפוחי אדמה	ta-POO-heh ah-da-MA
Bread	לחם	LEH-hem
Mineral water	מי-מעין	May-ma-YAHN
Wine; beer	בירה; יין	YA-yeen; BEE-ra
Coffee; tea	תה; קפה	ka-FEH; teh
Milk	חלב	'ha-LAHV

*For numbers see page 213.

Dessert	קינוח	Kee-NOO-AKH
Delicious	טעים מאד	ta-YIM meh-OHD
Police	משטרה	meesh-ta-RA
Doctor	רופא	ro-FEH
Dentist	רופא שיניים	ro-FEH shee-NA-yim
Sick	חולה	kho-LEH
Pain	כאב	keh-EHV
Do you understand?	מבין	meh-VEEN
I don't understand	לא מבין	lo meh-VEEN (man speaking)
	לא מבינה	lo meh-veen-NA (woman speaking)
Slowly	לאט	leh-AHT
Possible	אפשר	ef-SHAR
What is this?	מה זה	ma ZEH

NUMBERS

Hebrew numbers have masculine and feminine forms. With nouns that are feminine in gender, for instance, the feminine form of the number is used ("one boat" is pronounced "ah-KHAHT see-

RA"). Feminine forms are given for 1 through 10 only.

	MASCULINE	FEMININE
0	ZEH-ro	ZEH-ro
1	eh-HAHD	ah-KHAHT
2	sh'NA-yim	sh'TA-yim
3	sh'lo-SHA	sha-LOSH
4	ahr-ba-AH	ar-BA
5	ha-mee-SHA	ha-MESH
6	shee-SHA	shesh
7	sheev-AH	SHEH-va
8	sh'mo-NA	shmo-NEH
9	teesh-AH	TEH-sha
10	ah-sa-RA	EH-ser
11	ah-KHAD ah SAR	
12	SH'NA-yim ah-SAR	
13	shlo-SHA ah-SAR	
14	ar-ba-AH ah-SAR	
15	kha-mee-SHA ah-SAR	
16	shee-SHA ah-SAR	

17	sheev-AH ah-SAR
18	shmo-NA ah SAR
19	teesh-AH ah SAR
20	es-REEM
21 (etc.)	es-RIM veh-eh-HAHD
30	shlo-SHEEM
40	ar-ba-EEM
50	kha-mee-SHEEM
60	shee-SHEEM
70	shee-VEEM
80	shmo-NEEM
90	teesh-EEM
100	meh-AH
1000	EH-lef
100,000	me-AH EH-lef
1,000,000	mil-YOHN

For Telling Time

The *feminine* form of the number word is used, since the word for "hour" (pronounced "sha-AH") is feminine.

What time is it?	Ma ha sha-AH?
It's one o'clock	Ha sha-AH ah-KHAHT
One ten	ah-KHAHT EH-ser
Half past one	at-KHAHT va-KHEH-tsee
It's two o'clock	ha sha-AH SHTA-yim

HEBREW

Hebrew is unique among languages—it is one that has come back from the past. Once spoken in ancient Judea, Hebrew is a linguistic descendant of Aramaic. With the dispersal of the Jewish population of Judea the language declined and then ceased to be an everyday spoken language, although it continued as a religious and literary one. After the reestablishment of Israel as a state, it once more became a living language for everyday use.

To express modern concepts that did not exist in ancient times, the Old Testament was frequently consulted. To translate "electricity," for example, a word was found in Ezekiel 1:14 describing the radiant halo around the Lord: *hashmal.* "Traffic light" is expressed by *ramzor,* which indicates a sign or hint of light. The word for "airplane," *aviron,* derives from the ancient word for "air," *avir.*

Ehud Benyehuda, a famous Hebrew scholar, was a child when his family settled after World War I in what is now Israel. His parents had learned the revived Hebrew and spoke it between themselves; most returning Jews, in contrast, spoke Yiddish or other languages. The child was confused because he could not understand other children with whom he came in contact. At the age of three he still did not speak at all. But he had a sort of pet, a harmless snake that lived in the rafters of the house. One day the boy pointed to the snake and said *ha nhachash* ("the snake" in Hebrew). His father, Eliezer, was equal to the occasion and said to his wife: "Hebrew has now been spoken as a natural language for the first time in almost two thousand years!" Thereafter Ehud learned rapidly and came to speak many languages. He learned Arabic faster than some other languages because of the similar words in Arabic and Hebrew that share Aramaic roots.

HEBREW WORDS YOU ALREADY KNOW

There are a number of Hebrew words in English, the majority from the Bible: *amen, hallelujah, rabbi, kosher* (*kasher*—"according to law"), *camel, ebony, sapphire,* and *cherub,* the last originally referring to a powerful and stern guardian (in Assyria, a winged human-faced bull), not a cupid. An interesting modern word from Hebrew is *sabra:* used to a person born in Israel, it means a kind of pear, rough on the outside but sweet on the inside.

SOME COMMON EXPRESSIONS

ba-ROOKH ha-BA (singular)	Welcome ("Blessed the coming")
broo-KHEEM ha-ba-EEM (plural)	Welcome
le KHA-yim	Your health! ("To life!")
KA-ma yahf-FEH	How beautiful
ma ko-REH	What's going on?
meh-ahn-YAHN meh-OHD	Very interesting
ma-ZAHL tohv	Congratulations
dree-SHAHT sha-LOHM	Best regards
ness-see-HA toh-VA	Have a good trip

Some terms of endearment:

ah-NEE oh-HEHV oh-TAKH	I love you (man to woman)
ah-NEE oh-HEH-veht oht-KHAH	I love you (woman to man)

ah-HOOV	Beloved (m)
ah-hoo-VA	Beloved (f)

And otherwise:

ah-TSOHR	Stop!
ah-ZOHV oh-TEE	Don't bother me! (said by a man)
eez-VEE oh-TEE	Don't bother me! (said by a woman)
lekh mee-KAHN	Get lost! (to a man)
leh-KHEE mee-KAHN	Get lost! (to a woman)

Arabic	عربي	a'AH-ra-bi
Good day	السلام عليكم	al sa-lahm a'a-LAY-koom
Good evening	مساء الخير	MA-sa' el-KHAIR
How are you?	كيف حالكَ ؟ كيف حالكِ ؟	kaif HA-lak (m) kaif HA-lik (f)
Very well	مبسوط	mahb-SOOT
Happy to meet you	سعيد بلقائك	sa-e'ed BI-le-ka ak (m) sa-e'ed BE-le-ka ek (f)
Good bye	بخاطرك	BE-kha-trahk
My name	إسمي	is-mee
Your name	إسمك	is-MOOK-ka (m) is-MEH-kee (f)
Mr. (and) Mrs.	سيد أو سيدة	sa-YID (wa) sa-YEE-da
Miss	آنسة	AH-ne-sa
Yes	نعم	na-a'am
No; not	لا	la; mish
Excuse me	اسمح لي	is-MA-leh

Please	من فضلَك	min-FAHD-lak (m)
	من فضلِك	min-FAHD-lik (f)
Thank you	شكرا	shook-RAHN
You're welcome	عفوا	A'AF-wan
Again	ثانية	tha-NE-yah-tahn
Wait	انتظر	en-TA-zer (m)
	انتظري	en-TA-zeh-ree (f)
Enough	كفى	ka-fa
Where is	و ين	wehn
the tele-phone	التلفون	et teh-leh-FOHN
the toilet	الحمام	el ha-MAHM
the airport	المطار	el ma-TAR
the train station	محطة القطار	ma-HA-tet el ke-tar
the subway	النفق	el na-FAK
my baggage	شنطي	shoo-na-TEE
the train for ____	القطار إلى	el ke-TAR IL-la ____
the bus for ____	الباص إلى	al bahss IL-la ____

the boat for ___	الباخرة إلى ___	BA-khe-ra IL-la ___
What time?	قديش الساعة ؟	'ad-DESH-es sa-a'a
Now; not now	الآن ؛ ليس الآن	el an; LEH-sa el an
Later	بعدين	ba'a-DEYN
A bank	البنك	el bank
A drugstore	الصيدلية	al-SAI da-LEE-ya
A taxi stand	موقف التكسي	MAU-kef al-TA-xi
A market	السوق	al-sook
A department store	محل	ma-HAL
Far; not far	بعيد ؛ ليس بعيد	ba-E'ED; leh-sa ba-E'ED
Left; right	اليسار؛ اليمين	ya-SAR; ya-MIN
Here; there	هنا ؛ هناك	HO-na; ho-NAHK
Open; closed	افتح ؛ سكر	maf-TOOH; mogh-LAK
Beautiful	جميل	ja-MEEL
How much	كم	kahm

Very expensive	غالي	GRA-le
Less expensive	رخيص	re-khiss
Another color	لون آخر	laun AH-khar
Larger	أكبر	akh-BAR
Smaller	أصغر	as-GHAR
Hotel	فندق	fon-DOK
A room (with bath)	غرفة (مع حمام)	GHOR-fa (ma'a ha-MAHM)
Today	اليوم	al yohm
Tomorrow	غداً	GHA-dahn
____ days*	ــ أيام	____ ay-yam
What number?	شو الرقم ؟	shoo al-RA-kahm
Good; not good	كويس؛ مش كويس	KWOY-yis; mish-KWOY-yis
A restaurant	مطعم	ma-TAAM
Soup	شوربة	SHO-ra-ba
Meat	لحم	LA-hem
Chicken	دجاج	DA-jahj
Fish	سمك	SA-mak
Eggs	بيض	bide
Vegetables	خضرة	KHO-dra

*For numbers see page 225.

Rice	رز	rohz
Bread	خبز	KHOO-biz
Mineral water	میه معدنیة	MA-ya Ma'a-da-NEh-ya
Wine; beer	خمرة؛ بیرة	KHAHM-ra; BEE-ra
Coffee; tea	شاي؛ قهوة	KA-wa; shai
Milk	حلیب	HA-lib
Dessert	تحلایة	TEH-la-ya
Delicious	طیب کثیر	TAY-yib keh-tir
Police	البولیس	el bo-LISS
Doctor	طبیب	ta-BIB
Dentist	طبیب اسنان	ta-BIB ahss-naan
Sick	مریض	ma-RID
Pain	ألم	AH-lahm
Do you understand?	أتفهم؟	ah-TAHF-ham
I don't understand	أنا مش فاهم	AN-na mish FA-hem
Slowly	شوي شوي	shwey ee shwey
Possible	ممکن	MUM-kin
What is this?	إیش هذا؟	shoo HA-da

NUMBERS

0	sefr
1	WA-hid
2	t'NANE
3	ta-la-ta
4	ar-ba'a
5	kham-sa
6	SIT-ta
7	SA-ba'a
8	TA-ma-n'ya
9	TISS-a'a
10	A'A-sha-ra
11	heh-DA-shar
12	itt-NA-shar
13	ta-laht-TA-shar
14	ar-ba'a-TA-shar
15	kha-mahss-TA-shar
16	sit-TA-shar
17	sa-ba'a-TA-shar
18	ta-mahn-TA-shar
19	tiss-a'a-TA-shar

20	e'esh-RIN
21 (etc.)	WA-hid u e'esh-RIN
30	TA-la-tin
40	ar-ba-E'EN
50	kham-SEEN
60	sit-TEEN
70	sahb-E'EN
80	ta-mahn-NIN
90	tiss-E'EN
100	MEE-ya
1,000	ahlf
100,000	mit-ahlf
1,000,000	mil-YOHN

The Arabic numeral system became known to Europeans as a result of the frequent and lengthy wars waged against the Moslems throughout the Mediterranean world, including Spain, France, and particularly the Holy Land. In Roman and medieval times, Europeans wrote numerals according to the Roman system, an arrangement using the letters I, V, X, L, C, D, and M. As the Roman Empire grew to encompass much of the Old World, the numerical system became inadequate for expressing the large numbers as needed; this has even been cited as one of the many reasons for the collapse of the empire.

One wonders whether without the introduction of Arabic numerals, easy to use compared with the complicated Roman system, contemporary civilization could have developed as it has. While people in most Arabic-speaking countries still use an older form of these figures (1 through 9, with a dot for 0), they readily recognize the modern "Arabic" numerals that are in general use. It is interesting to reflect that medieval Arab mathematicians were the first to produce a truly international communication system for all the peoples of the world.

For Telling Time

What time is it?	Shoo SA'ah
It's nine o'clock	SA'ah TISS-a'ah
It's one ten	WA-hid wa A'A-sha-ra
It's half past two	SA'ah it'NANE oo nooss
Twenty to ten	SA'ah hid'AHSH IL-la'ish-REEN
At six o'clock	Iss SA'ah SIT-teh

ARABIC

Arabic, like Hebrew descended from the Aramaic of the Near East, has been the vehicle for passing a wide array of ancient and medieval scientific knowledge down to modern times. It has contributed words to mathematics (*algebra, azimuth, cipher*), to medicine and chemistry (*alchemy, alcohol, asthma*), to food (*sugar*), and even to fox hunting. "Tally ho!" is an expression the Crusaders brought back from Palestine: it comes from the Arabic *Tala hon!*—"Come here!" In astronomy, 70 percent of the stars bear Arabic names.

Arabic, a national language in many countries of Asia and Africa, has well over 100 million native speakers. Different regions are influenced by local dialects, but from Morocco to Iraq people in a great sweep of nations speak essentially the same language. Because of its increasing international importance, Arabic has been made one of the six official languages of the United Nations.

Written and spoken Arabic have been held together by the Koran, the holy book of Islam transcribed in the seventh century A.D. The word *Islam* means "submission"—submission to the will of Allah. Mainly because of the Koran, the Arabic alphabet has resisted all attempts at romanization except in those Moslem areas where Arabic is a religious and not a national language, such as Turkey, Indonesia, and Malaysia.

Written Arabic has an alphabet with letter values comparable to our Roman alphabet, except that it is written and printed in a flowing, connected script where most of the letters have four forms. These variants come to 100 letters, depending on the position of the basic letters, whether in front, middle, or last place in a word, or written alone. The curving forms of the letters are so graceful that they have been used for centuries to embellish mosques and palaces. When you look at Arabic words transliterated in Roman script you will often see an apostrophe written within the word. This indicates a guttural sound, for which you should have a catch or slight sob in your voice at this point in the word.

SOME COMMON EXPRESSIONS

Ahlan wa sahlan	AH-lahn wa sa-LAHN	Welcome in peace
Ilhamdulillah	ill-HAHM-doo-LIL-lah	God be praised
Bismillah	biss-MIL-la	In the name of God
Inshalla	in-SHAHL-la	As God wills
Mashalla	ma-SHAHL-la	May God preserve
Fi sahi tahk	fee SA-hee TAHK	To your health
Shul akbar?	shu l'ak-BAR	What's new?
Ma hadas?	ma-HA-dahs	What's happening?

| Mabrook | ma-BROUK | Congratulations |
| Ma'a es salaam | ma'a ess sa-LAHM | Have a good trip ("Go in safety") |

When somebody wishes you "Peace," as in *"Salaam aleikum,"* you should reply, *"Wa aleikum es salaam"* ("And on you be peace").

Some words of admiration:

Habibi	ha-BEE-bee	My beloved
Hilweh ketir	HILL-way k'teer	Very beautiful
Ain el ghazal	ayn el gha-ZAHL	Eye of the gazelle (to describe beautiful female eyes)

And otherwise:

| Ya ibn el kelb | ya ibn el kelb | O son of a dog |

Swahili

Swahili	Kiswahili	kee-swa-HEE-lee

SEE THE PRONUNCIATION GUIDE ON PAGE 240.

Good day	Hujambo	hoo-JAHM-bo
Good evening	Habari za jioni	ha-BA-ree za jee-O-nee
How are you?	U hali gani?	oo HA-lee GA-nee
Very well	Njema	N'JEH-ma
Happy to meet you	U hali gani	oo HA-lee GA-nee
Good-bye	Kwaheri	kwa-HEH-ree
My name is	Jina langu ni	JEE-na LAHN-goo nee
Your name	Jina lako	JEE-na LA-ko
Mr. (and) Mrs.	Bwana (na) Bibi	BWA-na (na) BEE-bee
Miss	Binti	BEEN-tee

Yes	Ndiyo	N'DEE-yo
No; not	La; si *or* hata	la; see, HA-ta
Excuse me	Niwehe radi	nee-WEH-heh RA-dee
Please	Tafadhali	ta-fahd-HA-lee
Thank you	Asante	ah-SAHN-teh
You're welcome	Asante sana	ah-SAHN-teh SA-na
Again	Tena	TEH-na
Wait	Ngoja	N'GO-ja
Enough	Imetosha	ee-meh-TOH-sha
Where is ____	____ Ipo wapi?*	____ EE-po WA-pee
the telephone	simu	SEE-moo
the toilet	choo	choo
the airport	kiwanja cha ndege	kee-WAHN-ja cha n'DEH-geh
the train station	stesheni ya gari le moshi	STEH-sheh-nee ya GA-ree la MO-shee

*"*Ipo wapi*" comes after the word for the place or thing asked about.

a bicycle	baisikeli	by-see-KEH-lee
my baggage	mizigo yangu	mee-ZEE-go YAHN-goo
the train for ____	gari la moshi kwa ____	GA-ree la MO-shee kwa ____
the bus for ____	basi kwa ____	BA-see kwa ____
the boat for ____	mashua kwa ____	ma-SHOO-ah kwa ____
What time?	Saa ngapi?	SA-ah N'GA-pee
Now; not now	sasa; hata sasa	SA-sa; HA-ta SA-sa
Later	baadaye	ba'a-DA-yeh
A bank	banki	bahnk-ee
A drugstore	Duka la mwuza dawa	DOO-ka la M'WOO-za DA-wa
A taxi	Teksiring	TEK-see-ring
A market	Soko	SO-ko
A big store	Duka kubwa	DOO-ka KOOB-wa
Far; not far	Mbali; karibu	M'BA-lee; ka-REE-boo

Left; right	Kushoto; kulia	koo-SHO-toh; KOO-lee-ya
Here; there	Hapa; huko	HA-pa; HOO-ko
Open; closed	Wazi; hufungwa	WA-zee; hoo-FOON-gwa
Beautiful	Mzuri	M'ZOO-ree
How much?	Bei gani?	BEH-ee GA-nee
Very expensive	Ghali sana	GA-lee SA-na
Less expensive	Duni ghali	DOO-nee GA-lee
Another color	Rangi nyingine	RAHN-ghee n'yee-en-GHEE-neh
Larger	Kikubwa kuliko hiko	koo-KOOB-wa koo-LEE-ko HEE-ko
Smaller	Kidogo kuliko hiko	kee-DOH-go koo-LEE-ko HEE-ko
Hotel	Hoteli	ho-TEH-lee
A room (with bath)	Chumba (kwa maji ya kuoga)	CHOOM-ba (kwa MA-jee ya KOO-O-ga)

Today	Leo	LEH-yo
Tomorrow	Kesho	KEH-sho
____ days*	____ siku	____ SEE-koo
What number?	Namba ngapi?	NAM-ba N'GA-pee
Good; not good	Kizuri; hata kizuri	kee-ZOO-ree; HA-ta kee-ZOO-ree
A restaurant	Hoteli	ho-TEH-lee
Soup	Supu	SOO-poo
Meat	Nyama	n'YA-ma
Chicken	Kuku	KOO-koo
Fish	Samaki	sa-MA-kee
Egg(s)	Yai	ya'ee
Vegetables	Mboga	M'BO-ga
Potatoes	Viazi	V'YA-zee
Bread	Mkate	MKA-teh
Mineral water	maji	MA-jee
Beer	Pombe	POHM-beh
Coffee; tea	Kahawa; chai	ka-HA-wa; chai
Milk	Maziwa	ma-ZEE-wa

*For numbers see page 236.

Dessert	Tamu-tamu	TA-moo-TA-moo
Very good	Kizuri sana	kee-ZOO-ree SA-na
Police	Mapolisi	ma-po-LEE-see
Doctor	Daktari	dahk-TA-ree
Dentist	Daktari wa meno	dahk-TA-ree wa MEH-no
Sick	Mgonjwa	MGOHN-j'wa
Pain ("It is painful")	Inauma	ee-na-OO-ma
Do you understand?	Unafahamu?	oo-na-fa-HA-moo
I don't understand	Sifahamu	see-fa-HA-moo
Slowly	Polepole	PO-leh-PO-leh
Possible	Inawezekana	ee-na-weh-zeh-KA-na
What is this?	Hi ni nini?	hee nee NEE-nee

NUMBERS

0	si kitu	see-KEE-too
1	moja	MO-ja

2	mbili	MBEE-lee
3	tatu	TA-too
4	nne	n'neh
5	tano	TA-no
6	sita	SEE-ta
7	saba	SA-ba
8	nane	NA-neh
9	tisa	TEE-sa
10	kumi	KOO-mee
11	kumi na moja	KOO-mee na MO-ja
12	kumi na mbili	KOO-mee na MBEE-lee
13	kumi na tatu	KOO-mee na TA-too
14	kumi na nne	KOO-mee na n'neh
15	kumi na tano	KOO-mee na TA-no
16	kumi na sita	KOO-mee na SEE-ta
17	kumi na saba	KOO-mee na SA-ba
18	kumi na nane	KOO-mee na NA-neh

19	kumi na tisa	KOO-mee na TEE-sa
20	ishirini	ee-shee-REE-nee
21	ishirini na moja	ee-shee-REE-nee na MO-ja
30	thelathini	theh-la-THEE-nee
40	arobaini	ah-ro-ba-EE-nee
50	hamsini	hahm-SEE-nee
60	sitini	see-TEE-nee
70	sabini	sa-BEE-nee
80	themanini	theh-ma-NEE-nee
90	tisini	tee-SEE-nee
100	mia	MEE-ya
1000	elfu moja	EL-foo MO-ja
100,000	mia elfu	MEE-ya EL-foo
1,000,000	milioni	meel-YO-nee

For Telling Time

Except in larger cities, speakers of Swahili divide the twenty-four hours of the day into two twelve-hour segments: light starts at dawn, or *asabuhi,* which is 6 A.M., and darkness, or *jioni,* at 6 P.M. This system has proven effective for hunters and farmers, indicating as it does light and darkness, which occur with little time variation in the central areas of Africa.

What time is it?	Sa'a ngapi?	SA-ah ng-AH-pee
Eight A.M. (two hours of daytime)	Sa'a mbili asabuhi	SA-ah MBEE-lee ah-sa-BOO-hee
Ten P.M. (four hours of nighttime)	Sa'a nne jioni	SA-ah nay jee-OH-nee
Midnight (six hours of nighttime)	Sa'a sita jioni	SA-ah SEE-ta jee-OH-nee
Half past eight (either A.M. or P.M.; it must be qualified)	Sa'a nane na nusu	SA-ah NA-nay na NOO-soo

SWAHILI

Swahili started as a trade language on the East Coast of Africa several hundred years ago and slowly spread inland. Kiswahili (literally, "tongue of the coast") is primarily a Bantu language with a certain amount of Arabic mixed in. It is now written in Roman letters and is spoken in Kenya, Uganda, Tanzania, the Congo, Zimbabwe, Burundi, Zaire, and other countries in East and Central Africa. The word *Bantu* itself is used in language studies to classify a number of South and Central African languages. In Bantu languages the word for "man" sounds like *mtu. Ba* (or *wa*), placed before the noun, indicates a plural. Thus *Bantu* means "the men."

Swahili words are easy to pronounce. The vowels *a, e, i, o,* and *u* are pronounced "ah," "eh," "ee," "oh," and "oo." In a two-syllable word stress the first syllable: JAM-bo (hello). In a longer word stress the next-to-the-last syllable: Kwa-HEH-ri (good-bye). The only slight difficulty for foreigners is pronouncing combinations such as *mb, mz, nd,* and *nj.* Even this isn't too hard if we imagine an apostrophe between the consonants, as is shown in the phonetic spelling in the third column. It's linguistically unusual for English-speakers, but it is not difficult.

Swahili's simple pronounciation is one reason for its increasing use through southeast and central Africa, and indicates that it is on its way to becoming an important world language.

SWAHILI WORDS YOU ALREADY KNOW

Because a number of independent African nations were once British colonies, some Swahili words are

familiar to English-speaking people. These include
bwana (master), *safari* (trip), and in politics,
uhuru (independence). Swahili words based on English ones include *hoteli* (hotel or restaurant),
menu, supu (soup), *baa* (bar), *gilasi* (glass), *dansi*
(dance), *siteki* (steak), *karati* (carrots), *letasi saladi*
(lettuce salad), *keki* (cake), *ais krimu* (ice cream),
baisikeli (bicycle), *motokari* (car), *tiketi* (ticket),
stesheni (station), *petroli* (gasoline), and *jipi* (jeep).

SOME COMMON EXPRESSIONS

Unasema Kiswahili?	U-na-SEH-ma kee-swa-HEE-lee	Do you speak Swahili?
Unasema Kiingeresa?	U-na-SEH-ma kee-in-geh-REH-sa	Do you speak English?
Wewe umetoka wapi?	weh-weh oo-meh-TOH-ka wa-pee	Where are you from?
Karibu	ka-REE-boo	Welcome; Come in
Kwa siha yako!	kwa SEE-ha ya-ko	To your health!
Hongera!	hon-GHEH-ra	Congratulations!
Unapenda?	oo-na-PEN-da	Do you like it?

| Bahati njema | ba-HA-tee n'JEH-ma | Good luck |

Some special expressions for photography or hunting:

Pole pole	PO-lay PO-lay	Slowly
Simile	si-MEE-lay	Look out
Sasa	sa-sa	Now
Haraka	ha-RA-ka	Hurry
Fisi	FEE-see	Hyena
Nati	NA-tee	Buffalo
Kiboko	kee-BO-ko	Hippo
Tembo	TEM-bo	Elephant
Chui	choo'ee	Leopard
Simba	SIM-ba	Lion

And for making friends:

Twende sinema	TWEN-dee SEE-neh-ma	Let's go to the movies
Mzuri sana	MZUR-ee SA-na	Very beautiful
Ume pendeza	OO-may pen-DEH-za	You are charming (m)

| We mrembo | WAY mrem-bo | You are charming (f) |

And otherwise:

| Vee stay gloop | vee stay gloop | You are a fool |

Hindi	हिन्दी	HIN-dee
Good day	नमस्ते	na-ma-STEH
Good evening	नमस्ते	na-ma-STEH
How are you?	आप कैसे हैं ?	ahp-KHAI-sah hay
Very well	अच्छा	ah-cha
Happy to meet you	आप को मिल के खुशी हुई	ahp ko MIL-keh KOO-sheeh'wee
Good-bye	फिर मिलेंगे	Peer-meh-LEN-gay
My name	मेरा नाम	MEH-ra naahm
Your name	आपका नाम	AHP-ka-naahm
Mr.(&) Mrs.	श्रीमान(और) श्रीमति	SHREE-man (our) SHREE-mat-tee
Miss	कुमारी	Koo-MA-ree
Yes	हाँ	haa
No; not	ना; नहीं	na;na-HEENH
Excuse me	माफ़	Ma-ahf
Please	कृमया	Kroo-PEH-ya
Thank you	शुक्रिय:	Shoo-KREE-ya
You're welcome	आप का स्वागत है	AHP-ka-SWA-gut hay

Again	फिर से	Peer-seh
Wait	इन्तज़ार	In-teh-zar
Enough	बहुत हैं	ba-HOOT hay
Where is	कहां हैं	ka-HAHN hay
The telephone	टेलीफोन	teh-leh-FOON
The toilet	शौंचालय	so-chlay-AH
The Airport	हवाई अड्डा	ha-WAI-AH-dda
The train station	रेलवे स्टेशन	"railway station
A bicycle	साईकिल	SAI-kal
My baggage	मेरा सामान	MEH-ra-SA-mahn
The train for--	--को जाने वाली गाड़ी	kee GA-ree
The bus for--	--को जाने वाली बस	kee bahss
The boat for--	--को जाने वाली नौव	kee na'oh
What time?	कया समय	k'ya sa-May
Now; not now	अभी; अभी नहीं	ah-BEE; ah-Bee naHEENH
Later	बाद में	BAHD-mee
A bank	बैंक	bank
A drug store	दवाईयों की दुकान	da-wa-KEE doo-KAHN
A taxi	टैक्सी	TA-k' see
A market	बाज़ार	BaZaar

A department store	बड़ी दुकान	ba-DEE doo-KAHN
Far; not far	दूर; दूर नहीं	dur; dur na-HEENH
Left; right	बाँय; दायँ	BA-yeh; DA-yeh
Here; There	इधर; उधर	ID-her; ooD-her
Open; closed	खुला; बन्द	KOO-la; band
Beautiful	सुन्दर	SOON-der
How much?	कितना	KEET-na
Expensive	बहुत महंगा	ba-HOOT-men-GA
Less expensive	सस्ता	So-sta
Another color	दुसरा रंग	DOO-seh-ra-RAHN-ga
Larger	बहुत बड़ा	ba-HOOT ba-DA
Smaller	बहुत छोटा	ba-HOOT cho-TA
Hotel	होटल	ho-TEL
A room (with bath)	कमरा (स्नानघर के साथ	KHAM-ra (SNAHN-ger keh-SAT)
Today	आज	ahj
Tomorrow	कल	kahl
--Days	--दिन	--deen
What number	क्या नंबर	k'ya NAHM-bar
Good; not good	अच्छा; अच्छा नहीं	aht-CHA; aht-CHA na-HEENH

A restaurant	रेस्टोरन्ट	res-toh-RAHNT
Soup	सूप	Soop
Meat	मांस	mahnz
Chicken	मुरगी	mur-GHEE
Fish	मछली	ma-CHEE
Egg	अंडा	ahn-DA
Vegetables	सब्ज़ी	SAHB-jee
Rice	चावल रोटी	CHA-wahl
Bread	रोटी	RO-tee
Beer	बियर	BEE-yar
Coffee; tea	काफ़ी; चाय	KA-feh; chai
Milk	दुघ	doodh
Dessert	मिठाई	meet-HAI
Delicious	बहुत अच्छा	baa-HOOT AH-cha
Doctor	डाक्टर	DAHK-ter
Dentist	दांत के डाक्टर	DANT-keh DAHK-ter
Sick	बीमार	bee-MAR
Pain	दुख	dookh
Do you understand?	आप समझे	ap sohm-jeh
I don't understand	मैं नहीं समझता	meh na-HEE so-ma-JTA

Slowly	धीरे धीरे	DEE-reh DEE-reh
Possible	संभव	soome-BOW
What is this?	ये क्या हैं ?	yeh g'ya hai

NUMBERS

0	see-far
1	ehk
2	doh
3	teen
4	chahr
5	pahnch
6	ch'heh
7	saht
8	ahth
9	now
10	dahss
11	G'YA-ra
12	BA-ra
13	TEH-ra
14	CHOW-da

15	PAHN-dra
16	SO-la
17	SAHT-ra
18	AHT-ha-ra
19	oon-NEES
20	EHK-beess
21	EHK-ees
30	tees
40	cha-LEES
50	pa-CHAHS
60	sahth
70	saht-TAHR
80	AHS-see
90	na-VEH
100	sow
1,000	ha-ZAHR
100,000	ehk lahkh
1,000,000	dahss lahkh

While Arabic numerals are now used worldwide, it is worth noting that the decimal system was first developed in ancient India. From India it was adopted by the Arab world and thence filtered into Europe. Eventually, with modified symbols for the numbers we use today, the British brought it back to India, where it had started. No one knows what ancient mathematician invented the decimal system, but thousands of years ago the cultures of India and Babylonia were able to express and use numbers in the millions and billions, something the ancient Romans and Greeks were unable to do.

For Telling Time

What time is it?	KIT-meh BA-jeh hay
It's seven o'clock	Saht BA-jeh hay
It's ten past seven	Saht BAJ-keh dahss MIN-at
A quarter to two	PA-neh doh BA-jeh
A quarter past two	SA-wa doh BA-jeh
It's half past eight	SAR-keh ahth BA-jeh hay

HINDI

The languages Hindi and Urdu are very closely related, and both descended from Hindustani, a language of central and northern India which was spoken by several hundred million people. Hindi is now the principal language of India, while Urdu is the main language of Pakistan. The word *Urdu* is related to the English word *horde;* in India, at the time of the Mogul emporers, it meant "army." It was the conquering Mogul armies who helped spread this version of Hindustani, with a number of Persian words, over India.

Both Hindi and Hindustani are written in special letters called Devanagari ("writing of the gods"); this term recalls the Sanskrit writings of ancient times. Urdu is written in the Arabic alphabet.

The fourteen languages printed on paper currency in India are among the most important of the many spoken there. Each is used by millions of people, but Hindi will serve you over the greater part of the peninsula, except in parts of the far south.

You are doubtless familiar with a number of Hindustani words that have entered English through the long association of Great Britain with India, many of them reminiscent of the good life led by the British Raj. These include *khaki, seersucker, chintz, bungalow, verandah, punch* (so called because of its five, *panch,* ingredients), *curry, polo, rajah,* and in a more sinister connection, *thug, loot,* and *suttee* (self-immolation by a widow).

SOME COMMON EXPRESSIONS

Ahp ka-HAHN   Where are you from?
say hay

MEH-reh g'har ko ahp-NA g'hahr SA-mahj-yeh	Make yourself at home
Ba-HOOT deel-CHAHSP	Very interesting
JAHL-dee ka-RO	Hurry up
Moo-BA-rahk ho	Congratulations
Ah-DAHB-keh-saht	Best regards
DEH-ko	Look
Ba-HOOT hay	Enough

And for making friends:

Ahp kee ba-REE meh-hehr-BA-nee	You are very kind
Kit-NA k'hoob-soo-RAHT	How beautiful
Moo-BAR-ek Sa far HO	Have a good trip

And otherwise:

MOOD-JAH na-HEENH sa-TA-oh	Don't bother me
NEE-kahl j'ow	Get out

CHINESE
(Mandarin)

Chinese	中文	zhōg-wén

NOTE: Chinese uses four tones to differentiate between syllables that have different meanings. You will find these tones designated in the third column over the syllables: ‾ indicates a high flat tone; ´ indicates a tone that starts low, then rises; ˇ indicates a tone that starts high, falls, then rises; ` indicates a tone that starts high, then falls; no mark indicates a neutral tone. The Chinese words are transliterated here into Roman letters according to the pinyin system; see page 262 for further pronunciation instructions.

Good day	你好	něe hǒw
Good evening	晚安	wǎhn āhn
How are you?	你好嗎	něe hǒw ma
Very well	很好	hǔn hǒw
Happy to meet you	久仰大名	jǒ yǎhng dà míng
Good-bye	再見	dz'ài j'yèn
My name	我的名字	wǒ-duh míng-d'zih

Your name	你貴姓	něe gwày-shìng
Mr. (and) Mrs.	先生　和　太太	sh'yēn-shūng (huh) tài-tai
Miss	小姐	sh'ow j'yěh
Yes	是	shìh
No; not	不；不是	bòo; bòo shìh
Excuse me	對不起	d'wày bòo chěe
Please	請	chǐng
Thank you	謝謝你	sh'yèh-sh'yèh něe
You're welcome	不客氣	bòo-kèh-chèe
Again	再	dz'ài
Wait	等	dǔng
Enough	夠了	gò-lā
Where is (it)?	在那裏	dz'ài nǎ lěe
the telephone		d'yèn hwà
the toilet	洗手間	shěe shǒ j'yen
the airport	飛機場	fēy jēe chǎhng

the train station	火車站	hwó chūh jàhn
a bicycle	自行車	d'zìh shíng chūh
my baggage	我的行李	wŏ-duh shíng-lĕe
the train for ＿＿＿	往　的火車	wăng ＿＿＿-duh huó-chūh
the bus for ＿＿＿	往　的公車	wăng ＿＿＿-duh gōong-chūh
the boat for ＿＿＿	往　的船	wăng ＿＿＿-duh ch'wén
What time?	幾點？	jée d'yĕn
Now; not now	現在；不是現在	sh'yĕn dz'ăi; bòo shìh sh'yĕn dz'ăi
Later	以後	yĕe hò
A bank	銀行	yín háhng
A drugstore	藥房	yòw fáhng
A taxi stand	計程車站	jèe-chúng-chūh-d'yèn

A market	市場	shìh-chǎhng
A department store	百貨店	bái-hwò-d'yèn
Far; not far	遠；不遠	yoo'wěn; bòo yoo'wěn
Left; right	左；右	tswǒ; yò
Here; there	這裏；那裏	chùh-lěe; nà lěe
Open; closed	開；關	kāi; gwan
Beautiful	美麗	mǎy-lèe
How much?	多少？	dwō-sh'ǒw
Very expensive	很貴	hǔn gwèy
Less expensive	不很貴	bù hǔn gwèy
Another color	別的顏色	b'yéh-duh yén-sèh
Larger	大一點	dà ee d'yěn
Smaller	小一點	sh'ǒw ee d'yěn
Hotel	旅館	lǘ-guǎn
A room (with bath)	房間 有洗澡間	fáhn-j'yen (yǒ shěe ts'ǒw j'yēn)
Today	今天	chīn t'yén

Tomorrow	明天	míng t'yén
____ days*	天	____ t'yén
What number?	幾號?	chĕe hòw
Good; not good	好;不好	hŏw; boo hŏw
A restaurant	飯館	fàhn-gwăhn
Soup	湯	tahng
Meat	肉	rò
Chicken	鷄	jēe rò
Fish	魚	yǘ
An omelet	荷包蛋	húh-b'ōw-dāhn
Vegetables	蔬菜	shū-ts'ài
White rice	白飯	bái fàhn
Noodles	麵	m'yèn
Bottled water	一瓶水	yée píng shwăy
Wine (or) beer	酒 和 啤酒	j'yŏ (húh) pée-j'yŏ
Tea (or) coffee	茶 和 咖啡	chá (húh) kā-fēi
Milk	牛奶	n'yú-năi
Dessert	甜點	d'yĕn-shīn

*For numbers see page 258.

Delicious	好吃	hǒw chīh
Police	警察	jǐng-chá
Doctor	醫生	yēe shūng
Dentist	牙醫	yá-yēe
Sick	生病	bìng-luh
Pain	痛	túng
Do you understand?	你明白嗎？	něe míng-bái ma
I don't understand	我不明白	wǒ bòo míng-bái
Slowly	慢慢	màhn-mahn
Possible	可以	kěh-yée
What is this?	這是什麼？	chùh shìh shén-muh

NUMBERS

0	lìng
1	yée
2	èr
3	sāhn
4	sìh
5	wǒo

6	l'yò
7	chēe
8	bā
9	j'yŏ
10	shíh
11	shíh-yée
12	shíh-èr
13	shíh-sāhn
14	shíh sìh
15	shíh wŏo
16	shíh l'yò
17	shíh-chēe
18	shíh-bā
19	shíh-j'yŏ
20	èr-shíh
21	èr-shíh yée
30	sāhn-shíh
40	sìh-shíh
50	wŏo-shíh
60	l'yò-shíh
70	chēe-shíh
80	bā-shíh

90	j'yò-shíh
100	băi
1,000	ch'yen
10,000	wàn
100,000	shíh-wàn
1,000,000	băi-wàn

Dangerous Numbers

An account of the building of the Great Wall of China tells of a prophecy that Qin Shi Huang-ti, the first emperor of the Qin dynasty, could not finish the wall until "ten thousand" had died and been buried in it. Rather than wait, the emperor ordered a man by the name of Wan, which sounded like "ten thousand" (except for the tone), executed and built into the wall.

Along the same lines, Chinese customarily refuse to accept license plates bearing 14-14, with good reason: in Chinese, the words for "fourteen fourteen" sound like the words for "certain death, certain death."

For Telling Time

What time is it?	Jée-d'yĕn jōhng
Eight o'clock	Bā d'yĕn jōhng
Half past eight	Bā d'yĕn bàhn

Nine o'clock	J'yŏ d'yĕn jōhng
Ten past three	Sāhn d'yĕn shíh jōhng
At what time?	Shén-muh shíh hò?

CHINESE

The term *Mandarin* (the Western word for the northern Chinese dialect and now the national language) stems from a time when the mandarins were the ruling class of China. Hundreds of years ago, seafaring Portuguese arrived in China and asked the populace who their leaders were. The Chinese responded, "Manchu people" (*manchu-ren*). The Portuguese thought the Chinese were identifying themselves as Manchurian, and the name has survived to this day even though the Manchu conquerers have long since disappeared or been assimilated.

The Chinese name for their now unified language is *guo-yü,* "the country's language," or *chung-guo hua,* "the central country talk." Both terms suggest that China is the center and most important part of the world. In a sense it is, since the Chinese language is spoken by more than a billion people, who greatly outnumber the speakers of any other language.

Mandarin is not simple, and since the time of Marco Polo, Western travelers, missionaries, and businessmen have tried to render the thousands of beautiful but complicated Chinese characters in Roman letters, for Western pronunciation. Many of these transliterations have been incorrect. In the late 1940s, a special effort was begun to create a standardized spelling and pronunciation guide using the Roman alphabet. This relatively new adaptation, called pinyin, is now being taught in Chinese schools, and while it has not replaced the thousand-year-old Chinese characters, it is used in a number of cities on street signs and for the Western spelling of Chinese personal and place names.

This new romanized spelling has caused a certain havoc in libraries, newspaper-file rooms, and other collections with records going back hundreds of years. The older spelling "Peking," for instance, has been changed to "Beijing." The name is still the same, and still means "North Capital," but the spelling is closer to the true sound. Spellings of the names of other large Chinese cities have also changed; "Shanghai," however, which means "by the sea," is still written in the old way.

You will undoubtedly see a number of signs written in pinyin in China. In the first part of this chapter the words were spelled phonetically, but in the following part the words are written in pinyin so you can learn how to pronounce it. Certain letters have the same value as in English, but many letters (or combinations) are said differently. You can pronounce them correctly if you remember:

an is pronounced "un"

c is pronounced "ts"

e is pronounced "uh"

eng is pronounced "ung"

ie is pronounced "yeh"

ian is pronounced "yen"

iu is pronounced "eo"

j is pronounced "zh"

g is pronounced "eh"

ii is pronounced as if you were saying "ee" with the lips pursed in a tight circle

ui is pronounced "way"

uo is pronounced "waw"

x is pronounced "sh"

z is pronounced "dz"

zh is pronounced "j"

Chinese may be written several ways: horizontally left to right (as Western languages) or right to left. It can also be written vertically from top to bottom, and read right to left, with pages running "backward" (from the Western point of view), like Japanese, Hebrew, Arabic, and some other languages. But when Chinese is written in pinyin, the lines are *always* horizontal and read left to right.

The good news about Chinese is that it is easy to speak if you use the correct tones. There are no masculine or feminine forms, no verb variations, no tenses; grammatically, Chinese is even simpler than English.

The ancient Chinese characters are still very much in use, of course, although some have been simplified over the years to save time. The old writing is not only beautiful but also instructive. Consider the combination of characters to make a special meaning: "woman" plus "child" means "good"; "man" standing by "word" means "honesty"; "woman" plus "pig" under "roof" means "marriage"; a woman looking around a door means "jealousy"; and "small" plus "heart" means "Be careful!" (an admonition generally used at railway crossings).

SOME COMMON EXPRESSIONS

The following phrases are written in pinyin. NOTE: The combination *ai* is pronounced like the "ai" in "Shanghai."

Zhōng-guó huà ma?	jōng-gwó hwà ma	Do you speak Chinese?
Nǐ shì meǐ-guó rén?	nĕe shìh mǎy-gwó rén	Are you American?
Nǐ shì ying-guó rén?	nĕe shìh ying-gwó rén	Are you English?
Huān-yíng	hwāhn-yíng	Welcome

Nǐ yào shén-me?	něe yòw shén-muh	What do you wish?
Jìn zhǐ	jìn jeě	Forbidden
Shí bù shí?	shíh bòo shíh	Isn't it so?
Wǒ bù zhī-dào	wǒ bòo jēe-dòw	I don't know
Méi guān xì	Máy gwāhn shèe	It doesn't matter
Jiàn kāng	j'yèn kāhng	To your good health
Húi-lái	hwáy-lái	Come again

Some words of admiration:

Wǒ-de péng-yǒu	wǒ-duh púng-yǒ	My friend
Nǐ shì hěn hǎo-kàn	něe shìh hǔn hǒw-kàhn	You are very attractive
Aì rén	aì rén	Beloved

And otherwise:

| Bàn dàn | bàhn dàhn | Fool ("Stupid egg") |
| Guěn dàn | gwěn dàhn | Get lost ("Roll like an egg") |

| Wài gúo rén | wài gwó rén | Outside person ("Foreigner") |
| Yáng kuěi | yáhng kwǎy | Devil ocean ghost; (a term once used for pale-skinned Occidentals who, in the past, arrived in China from the ocean) |

JAPANESE

Japanese	日本語	nee-hon-go

NOTE: Traditionally Japanese is written in a vertical column, from top to bottom. Columns are read from right to left on a page. Japanese can also be written horizontally, as has been done here, in which case it is usually read from left to right, like English. A line over a vowel should be prolonged slightly. Otherwise Japanese syllables have equal emphasis, except for those with "u," whose sound is often minimized or elided. See also page 276. The syllable "hai" is pronounced like the English word "high".

Good day	今日は	ko-nee-chee-wa
Good evening	今晩は	kohn-ban wa
How are you?	いかがですか？	ee-ka ga-dess-ka
Very well	元気です	gen-kee dess
Happy to meet you	始めまして	ha-jee-meh-ma-sh´teh
Good-bye	さようなら	sa-yo-na-ra
My name	私の名前	wa-tahk-shee-no na-ma´ee
Your name	貴方の名前	ah-na-ta-no na-ma´ee

Mr.; Mrs.; Miss	さん	-san (after name)
Yes	はい	hai
No; not	いいえ； ではありません	ēē-yeh; deh wa ar-ree-ma-sen
Excuse me	すみません	soo-mee-ma-sen
Please	どうぞ	dōh-zo
Thank you	有難う	ah-ree-ga-tōh
You're welcome	どういたしま して	dōh ee-ta-shee- ma-shee-teh
Again	また	ma-ta
Wait	待って	chot-toh
Enough	充分	ju-boon
Where is (it)	何処ですか	doh-ko dess-ka
the telephone	電話	den-wa
the toilet	お手洗	o-teh-ah-rai
the airport	空港	koō-kō
the train station	列車の駅	reh-sha-no eh-kee
the subway	地下鉄	chee-ka-tet-su
my baggage	私の荷物	wa-tahk-shee-no nee-mo-t´su

the train for __	__ 行の列車	__ ee-kee-no reh-sha
the bus for __	__ 行のバス	__ ee-kee-no ba-soo
the boat for __	__ 行の船	__ ee-kee-no foo-neh
What time?	何時ですか？	nahn-jee-dess-ka
Now; not now	今；今では ありません	ee-ma; ee-ma deh-wa ah-ree-ma-sen
Later	あとで	ah-toh deh
A bank	銀行	ghin-kō
A drugstore	薬局	yahk-yo-koo
A taxi stand	タクシーの 乗り場	ta-koo-shee-no no-ree-ba
A market	マーケット	mā-ket-toh
A department store	デパート	deh-pā-toh
Far; not far	遠い；遠くない	tōh´ee; tōh-koo-nai
Left; right	左；右	hee-da-ree; mee-ghee
Here; there	此処に； あそこに	ko-ko-nee; ah-so-ko-nee

Open; closed	開けて; 閉めて	ah-keh-teh; shee-meh-teh
Beautiful	美しい	oot-soo-koo-shēē
How much?	いくら？	ee-koo-ra
Very expensive	大変高い	tai-hen ta-kai
Less expensive	高くない	ta-ka-koo nai
Another color	他の色	ho-ka-no ee-ro
Larger	もっと大きい	mo-toh ōh-kee
Smaller	もっと小さい	mo-toh chēē-sai
Hotel	ホテル	ho-teh-roo
A room (with bath)	部屋 （とお風呂）	he-ya (toh o-foo-ro)
Today	今日	k'yo
Tomorrow	明日	ah-shee-ta
__ days*	__ 日	__ nee-chee
What number?	何番ですか？	nahm-bahn dess-ka
Good; not good	良い; 良くない	yo'ee; yo-koo nai
A restaurant	レストラン	reh-so-toh-rahn
Soup	スープ	soo-poo
Meat	肉	nee-koo

*For numbers see page 272.

Chicken	とり	toh-ree
Fish	魚	sa-ka-na
Eggs	卵	ta-ma-go
Vegetables	野菜	ya-sai
Rice	御飯	go-hahn
Bread	パン	pan
Water	水	mizu
Sake (or) beer	酒（又は）ビール	sa-keh (ma-ta-wa) bēē-roo
Tea; coffee	お茶；コーヒー	o-cha; kō-hēē
Milk	ミルク	mee-roo-koo
Dessert	デザート	deh-zā-toh
Delicious	おいしい	oh-ee-shee´ee
Police	巡査	joon-sa
Doctor	医者	ee-sha
Dentist	歯医者	hai-sha
Sick	病気	b´yō-kee
Pain	痛い	ee-tai
Do you understand?	解りますか？	wa-ka-ree-mahss-ka

I don't understand	解りません	wa-ka-ree-ma-sen
Slowly	ゆっくり	yook-koo-ree
Possible	出来ます	deh-kee-mahss
What is this?	何ですか？	nahn-dess-ka

NUMBERS

Although Japanese has had its own system of writing numbers for thousands of years, the international system of Arabic numerals is now in general use in Japan and is understood by everyone. (For an explanation of *roma-ji,* see page 276.)

	ROMA-JI	PHONETIC
0	rei	ray
1	ichi	ee-chee
2	ni	nee
3	san	sahn
4	shi *or* yotsu	shee; yoht-soo (see page 275)
5	go	go
6	roku	ro-koo
7	shichi	shee-chee
8	hachi	ha-chee

| 9 | ku | koo |
| 10 | ju | joo |

And now for some good news. There are only twelve separate names of numbers to remember. They are for the numbers from 1 to 10; 100; and 10,000. The other number words are all combinations or rearrangements of these basic words, as you will see when you examine the list below.

	ROMA-JI	PHONETIC
11	ju-ichi	joo-ee-chee
12	ju-ni	joo-nee
13	ju-san	joo-sahn
14	ju-shi	joo-shee
15	ju-go	joo-go
16	ju-roku	joo-ro-koo
17	ju-shichi	joo-shee-chee
18	ju-hachi	joo-ha-chee
19	ju-ku	joo-koo
20	ni-ju	nee-joo
21	ni-ju-ichi	nee-joo-ee-chee
30	san-ju	sahn-joo

40	shi-ju *or* yon-ju	shee-joo; yohn-joo
50	go-ju	go-joo
60	roku-ju	ro-koo-joo
70	shichi-ju	shee-chee-joo
80	hachi-ju	ha-chee-joo
90	kyu-ju	k'yoo-joo
100	hyaku	h'ya-koo
1,000	sen	sen
10,000	man	mahn
1,000,000	hyakuman	h'ya-koo-mahn

Former assurances aside, an old way of saying the first ten numbers is still occasionally employed in conversation, mostly for small quantities of things you use or buy. These are the original Japanese numbers, and while it's not necessary to learn them, it can be useful to recognize them. In *roma-ji* (see page 276) they are written:

1	hitotsu
2	futatsu
3	mitsu
4	yotsu
5	itsutsu

6	mutsu
7	nanatsu
8	yatsu
9	rokonutsu
10	tō

The regular word for "four," *shi* (shee), is often avoided in conversation in favor of *yotsu* (yohtsoo), from the series of ancient Japanese numbers listed above. The reason for the substitution is simple: *shi* also means "death."

For Telling Time

What time is it?	Nan-ji desuka?	nahn-jee dess-ka
It's one o'clock	Ichi-ji desu	ee-chee dess
It's half past one	Ichi-ji han desu	ee-chee hahn dess
Five past two	Ni-ji go fun sugi	nee-jee go foon soo-gee
Ten to three	San-ji ju fun mae	sahn-jee foon ma-yeh
At three o'clock	San-ji ni	sahn jee nee

JAPANESE

Japanese is written in three distinct scripts as well as the Roman alphabet: *hiragana,* a fluid one for verbal and adjectival conjunctions; *katakana,* a simplified version of *hiragana* used for foreign words and names; and *kanji,* which uses many ancient Chinese ideographs, and with which the preceding two are usually combined. One must memorize thousands of Chinese ideographs to be considered truly literate in *kanji,* but this doesn't seem to have kept Japan from becoming one of the most literate of nations.

Japanese script is usually written in a vertical column, top to bottom. Columns are read from right to left on a page. Japanese can also be written in a horizontal line, as has been done in the eighty-words section, in which case it is usually read from left to right, like English.

The Roman-letter spelling of Japanese is called, appropriately enough, *roma-ji,* and this is the version you see in English-language newspapers when Japanese names and places are mentioned. "Tokyo," for instance, is a *roma-ji* spelling. While *roma-ji* is useful for foreigners, it shows no sign of replacing written Japanese with its thousands of characters, used in all Japanese publications. Signs in Japan are written in a combination of *kanji* and *hiragana,* while *katakana* and *roma-ji* are used for foreign names or words.

In *roma-ji,* the vowels *a, e, i, o,* and *u* are pronounced "ah," "eh," "ee," "oh," and "oo," respectively. In conversation the final "u" sound is often minimized, but otherwise all syllables are pronounced with the same emphasis. The only written accent used in *roma-ji,* a line over a vowel, indicates that the vowel so marked should be prolonged. When speaking, both the Japanese and the Chinese have difficulty differentiating between our "l" and "r" sounds, although the Chinese seem to find the former less difficult. The Japanese, on the other hand, don't pronounce it at all, and therefore the "l" sound isn't included in the *roma-ji* approximation of the English alphabet.

From this point on, Japanese words will be written in *roma-ji* followed by a phonetic rendition.

Japanese is among the most orderly of languages; word function in the phrase or sentence, direction of motion, location, and use are all designated by written symbols and spoken sounds. Each such symbol is written after the word it refers to and, in *roma-ji,* is attached by a hyphen to that word.

wa or *ga* for subject

o for direct object

ni for indirect object

no for possessive

e for place to

kara for place from

de for means of performing action

ka to indicate a question

ne to indicate ". . . isn't it?" It is also a convenient conversational pause or stopgap.

To an English-speaker, word order in Japanese seems inverted. In Japanese one says, "The theater where is it?" instead of "Where is the theater?" One might wonder which is more logical linguistically. Japanese, it should be remembered, has been a spoken language much longer than English.

JAPANESE WORDS
YOU ALREADY KNOW

English words have been adopted into Japanese by the thousands, although they are sometimes hard to recognize. They often refer to business, sports, science, manufacturing, and Western styles of living. You can recognize them more easily if you suppress the pronunciation of the *"u"* sound in these words, which are presented here in *roma-ji*. Some are easy to recognize: *motosaikuru, tenisu, taipuriata, rajio, proguramu, takushii.*
    Others are more difficult to identify:

kisu	kiss
modan garu	modern girl
teribi	television
tornjisuta	transistor

sandoicchi	sandwich
kokuteru	cocktail
sarariman	salaried man
gorufu	golf

And then there are the baseball terms: *homuran, hitto, sturaiku,* and *autto.*

Some Japanese words sound exactly like English words but have different meanings. *Ha-ha,* for instance, refers to one's own mother, and *Ohio* means "Good morning."

Visiting Americans who encounter difficulty saying the polite Japanese phrase for "You're welcome," *do itashmashite* (dōh ee-tahsh-mahsh-tee), have frequently used a linguistic "almost sound-alike" such as the phrase (said rapidly) "Don't touch moustache."

Japanese has a number of alliterative and picturesque words that suggest the movements or sounds illustrating the concept:

giza-giza	zig-zag
zen-zen	never
chotto-chotto	one moment
shiba-shiba	often
gata-gata	noisy sounds

soro-soro	very slow movement
pika-pika	lightning
don-don	thunder; explosion

SOME COMMON EXPRESSIONS

Moshi moshi	mo-shee mo-shee	Hello (on telephone)
Sumimasen	soo-mee-ma-sen	Pardon me
Anone	ah-no-neh	(Said to attract attention)
Nihon-go-o hanashimasu-ka?	nee-hohn-go-o ha-na-shee-mahss-ka?	Do you speak Japanese?
Amerika-jin desu-ka?	ah-meh-ree-ka-jin dess-ka	Are you an American?
Eikoku-jin desu-ka?	eh-ko-koo-jin dess-ka	Are you English?
Yoku irrashai mashita	yo-koo ee-ra-shai mahsh-ta	Welcome
Banzai!	bahn-zai	Hurrah! ("Ten thousand years")

Kampai!	kahm-pai	To your health! ("Dry cup")
Doshimashita-ka?	doh-shee-mahsh-ta-ka	What's the matter?
So desu-ka?	so dess-ka	Is that so?
Mochiron	mo-chee-rohn	Of course
Dai jobu	dai jo-boo	Everything is okay
Ikimasho	ee-kee ma-sho	Let's go

Some words of endearment or admiration:

Koibito	ko'ee-bee-toh	Dear; darling; loved one
Anatawa miryoko teki desu	ah-na-ta-wa mee-r'yo-ko teh-kee dess	You are charming

And otherwise:

Baka	ba-ka	Fool; nitwit

Indonesian

Indonesian	Bahasa Indonesia	ba-HA-sa in-doh-NEH-s'ya

SEE THE PRONUNCIATION NOTE ON PAGE 291.

Good day	Selamat pagi	seh-LA-maht PA-gee
Good evening	Selamat malam	seh-LA-maht MA-lam
How are you?	Apa kabar?	AH-pa ka-BAR
Very well	Baik	bike
Happy to meet you	Selamat bertemu	seh-LA-maht ber-TEH-moo
Good-bye	Selamat djalan (said by person staying)	seh-LA-maht JA-lahn
	Selamat tinggal (said by person leaving)	seh-LA-maht TING-gahl

My name	Nama say	NA-ma SA-ya
Your name	Nama tuan (m)	NA-ma too-AHN
	Nama nyonya (f)	NA-ma N'YOHN-ya
Mr. (and) Mrs.	Tuan (dan) Nyonya	too-AHN (dahn) N'YOHN-ya
Miss	Nona	NO-na
Yes	Ya	ya
No; not	Tidak	TEE-dahk
Excuse me	Ma'af	ma-ahf
Please	Tjoba	CHO-ba
Thank you	Terima kasi	teh-REE-ma KA-see
You're welcome	Kembali	kem-BA-lee
Again	Sekali lagi	seh-KA-lee LA-ghee
Wait	Tunggu	TOON-goo
Enough	Tjukup	CHOOK-up
Where is	Dimana	dee-MA-na
the telephone	telepon	teh-leh-POHN

the toilet	kamar ketchil	KA-mar ket-CHIL
the airport	pelabuhan terbang	peh-la-BOO-hahn TEHR-bang
the train station	stasion kereta-api	sta-S'YUHN keh-REH-ta-AH-pee
the bicycle	sepeda	seh-PEH-da
my baggage	barang barang saya	BA-rahng BA-rahng SA-ya
the train for _____	kereta-api ke _____	keh-REH-ta-AH-pee keh _____
the bus for _____	bis ke _____	bis keh _____
the boat for _____	perahu ke _____	peh-reh-HOO keh _____
What time?	Jam berapa?	jom beh-RA-pa
Now; not now	Sekarang; tidak sekarang	seh-KA-rahng; TEE-dahk seh-KA-rahng
Later	Nanti	nahn-TEE
A bank	Bangk	bahngk

A drugstore	Toko obat	toh-ko OH-baht
A taxi	Taxsi	TAHK-see
A market	Pasar	PA-sar
A department store	Toko barang-barang	TOH-ko BA-rahng-BA-rahng
Far; not far	Jauh; tidak jauh	jow; TEE-dahk jow
Left; right	Kiri; kanan	KEE-ree; KA-nahn
Here; there	Disini; disitu	dee-SEE-nee; dee-SEE-too
Open; closed	Terbuka; tutup	tehr-BOO-ka; TOO-toop
Beautiful	Indah	EEN-dah
How much?	Berapa?	beh-RA-pa
Very expensive	Mahal sekali	MA-hahl seh-KA-lee
Less expensive	Mahal kurang	MA-hahl KOO-rahng
Another color	Warna jang lain	WAR-na yahng line
Larger	Besar lagi	beh-SAR LA-gee

Smaller	Ketchil lagi	ket-CHIL LA-gee
Hotel	Hotel	ho-TEL
A room (with bath)	Kamar (dengan kamar mandi)	KA-mar (DENG-ghan KA-mar MAHN-dee)
Today	Hari ini	HA-ree EE-nee
Tomorrow	Besok	BEH-sok
___ days*	___ hari	___ HA-ree
What number?	Apa nomor?	AH-pa NO-mor
Good; not good	Bagus; tidak bagus	ba-GOOSS; TEE-dahk ba-GOOSS
A restaurant	Restoran	res-toh-RAHN
Soup	Sop	sohp
Meat	Daging	DA-ghing
Chicken	Ayam	AH-yam
Fish	Ikan	EE-kahn

*For numbers see page 288.

Omelet	Telor dadar	teh-LOR DA-dar
Vegetables	Sajuran	sa-JOO-rahn
Rice	Nasi	NA-see
Bread	Roti	RO-tee
Mineral water	Air soda	ay'r SO-da
Beer	Bir	beer
Coffee; tea	Kopi; teh	KO-pee; teh
Milk	Susu	SOO-soo
Dessert	Tambul	TAHM-bool
Delicious	Enak sekali	EH-nak seh-KA-lee
Police	Polisi	po-LEE-see
Doctor	Doktor	DOK-tor
Dentist	Doktor gigi	DOK-tor GHEE-ghee
Sick	Sakit	SA-keet
Pain	Sakit	SA-keet
Do you understand?	Mengerti?	men-gher-TEE
I don't understand	Saya tidak mengerti	Sa-ya TEE-dahk men-gher-TEE

Slowly	pelan-pelan	p'lahn-p'lahn
Possible	Mungkin	MOONG-kin
What is this?	Apa ini?	AH-pa EE-nee

NUMBERS

0	nol	nohl
1	satu	SA-too
2	dua	DOO-ah
3	tiga	TEE-ga
4	ampat	AHM-paht
5	lima	LEE-ma
6	anam	AH-nahm
7	tudjuh	TOOD-joo
8	delapan	deh-LA-pahn
9	sembilan	sem-BEE-lahn
10	sepuluh	seh-POO-loo
11	sebelas	SEH-b'iahss
12	duabelas	DOO-ah-b'lahss
13	tigabelas	TEE-ga-b'lahss

14	empatbelas	EM-paht-b'lahss
15	limabelas	LEE-ma-b'lahss
16	enambelas	EH-nahm-b'lahss
17	tudjuhbelas	TOOD-joo-b'lahss
18	delapanbelas	de-LA-pahn-b'lahss
19	sembilanbelas	SEM-bee-lahn-b'lahss
20	duapuluh	DOO-ah-poo-loo
21 (etc.)	duapuluh satu	DOO-ah-poo-loo sah-too
30	tigapuluh	tee-ga-poo-loo
40	empatpuluh	em-paht-poo-loo
50	limapuluh	lee-ma-poo-loo
60	enampuluh	eh-nahm-poo-loo
70	tujuhpuluh	tood-joo-poo-loo

80	delapanpuluh	deh-la-pahn-poo-loo
90	sembilanpuluh	sem-bee-lahn-poo-loo
100	seratus	seh-ra-toos
1,000	seribu	seh-ree-boo
100,000	seratus seribu	seh-ra-toos seh-ree-boo
1,000,000	juta	joo-ta

For Telling Time

Pukul means "striking"; *djam* means "hour."

What time is it?	Pukul berapa?	PU-kul be-RA-pa
Two o'clock	Pukul dua	POO-kool DOO-ah
Two ten	Pukul dua sakul sepuluh menit	POO-kool DOO-ah SA-kul seh-POO-loo MEH-net
Half past two ("half three")	Setenga tiga	sen-TEN-ga TEE-ga
At seven o'clock	Pada djam tudjuh	PA-da jahm TOOD-joo

INDONESIAN

Indonesian, the language of the former Dutch East Indies, is a major world language with more than 100 million speakers. Another 10 million people speak Malay, which is closely related to Indonesian; Indonesian-speakers can often understand Malay-speakers, and vice versa. Indonesian has served to unite the various peoples of Indonesia, and even foreign visitors find it easy and pleasurable to speak this logical language. The grammar is not complicated and words are easy to pronounce. Here are a few rules:

1. The vowels *a, e, i, o,* and *u* are pronounced "ah," "eh," "ee," "oh," and "oo," respectively.

2. A final written and spoken *-ka* indicates a question.

3. The word *apa* also prepares the listener for a question.

4. There are no tenses. The Indonesian word for "already," *suda,* indicates the past, and the words for "tomorrow," "next week," and so on indicate the future.

5. The plural in writing is formed by adding the numeral 2, which indicates that the world must be repeated when spoken. "Man" is *orang;* "men" is *orang-orang,* written as *orang-2.*

6. Indonesian has several words for "you." *Saudara* to a man means "brother" and *saudari* to a woman means "sister." An older man is called *bung* ("uncle"). *Enkau* also means "you" but is less formal, while *Tuan,* "master," is considerably more formal and traditional.

Some Indonesian words may already be familiar to you, or their meanings easy to guess. These include *doktor, sakit* (sick), *listrik* (electric), *lampu* (lamp), *topi* (hat), *orangutan* ("man of the forest"), *amok* (temporarily and dangerously crazed), *telephon, glas, sigaret, kopi* (coffee), *teh* (tea), *benzin* (gasoline), and *menit* (minute). An Indonesian (and Malay) name still enjoying worldwide recognition is that of the famous spy Mata Hari (literally, "eye of the day" or "sun").

SOME COMMON EXPRESSIONS

Apa bitchara bahasa Indonesia?	AH-pa beet-CHA-ra ba-HA-sa in-doh-NEH-s'ya	Do you speak Indonesian?
Selamat	seh-LA-mat	Peace; good luck; con-gratulations
Selamat minum!	seh-LA-mat MEE-num	To your health! ("Peace while drinking")

Selamat tidut	seh-LA-mat TEE-dur	Good night ("Peace while sleeping")
Mau apa?	m'ow AH-pa	What do you wish?
Silakanla	see-LA-kahn-la	Go ahead; Help yourself
Awas!	AH-wahs	Look out!
Tunggu sebentar	TOON-goo seh-BEN-tar	Wait a minute
Apa kabar?	AH-pa ka-BAR	What's the news? What's happening? How are you?
Dilarang	dee-LA-rang	Forbidden
Wasalam	wa-sa-LAHM	Best regards
Kembali lagi	kem-BA-lee LA-ghee	Come again

For a friendly mood:

Engkau tjantik	EN-kow CHAHN-tik	You are charming
Saya suka enkau sekali	SA-ya SOO-ka EN-kow seh-KA-lee	I like you very much

And perhaps in a crowded marketplace:

Berhenti!	ber-HEN-tee	Stop!
Pergi keluar!	pehr-ghee KEH-loo-ar	Get lost!
Djangan gangu saya!	JAHN-gahn GAHN-goo SA-ya	Don't bother me!

Thai

NOTE: Thai writing goes from left to right, the same as English. There are several tones in Thai, the most important of which are indicated with accents over the appropriate syllables in the phonetic spellings throughout, as follows: ´ indicates a rising tone; ` indicates a falling tone; ^ indicates a high flat tone; ¯ indicates a low flat tone.

Hello	สวัสดี	sa-wa-DEE kráb (m)
	สวัสดี	sa-wa-DEE ka (f)
How are you?	คุณสบายดีหรือ?	kuhn sa-bai-DEE rû
Very well	สบายดี	sa-bai-DEE
Happy to meet you	ยินดีที่รู้จักคุณ	yin dee TÊE-róo-jàk kuhn
Good bye	สวัสดี	sa-wa-DEE
My name	ผมชื่อ (m); ดิฉันชื่อ (f)	pom chêw (m); dee-chan chêw (f)
Your name	คุณชื่อ	kuhn chêw
Mr.; Mrs; Miss	คุณ	kuhn (said *after* name)
Yes	ใช่ครับ (m); ใช่ค่ะ (f)	chaî-kráb (m); chaî-ká (f)

No	ไม่ครับ (m); ไม่ค่ะ (f)	maî-kráb (m); maî-ká (f)
Not	ไม่ใช่	mâi-chai
Excuse me	ขอโทษ	kōr tôt
Please	กรุณา	ga-RÓO-NA
Thank you	ขอบคุณ	khòb kuhn
You're welcome	ไม่เป็นไร	mâi pen rai
Again	ขอวีก	kaw-eèk
Wait	รอก่อน	raw gon
Enough	พอแล้ว	pôr lēo
Where is	__ อยู่ที่ไหน	__ yòo têe nāi
the telephone	โทรศัพท์	tóra sàp
the toilet	ห้องน้ำ	hohng na'am
the airport	สนามบิน	sa-nàm bin
the train station	สถานีรถไฟ	sa-tà-née rot-fai
a bicycle	จักรยาน	jàk-ra-yān
my baggage	กระเป๋าของฉัน	kra-bao kóng-PHOM (m) kra-bao kóng-CHÀN (f)
the train for __	รถไฟไป __	róht fāi bai __
the bus for __	รถเมล์ไป __	róht mey bai __

the boat for __	เรือไป __	rew-ah bai __
What time?	เวลาอะไร	wey-la arái?
Now; not now	เดี๋ยวนี้	d'yō née
	ไม่เดี๋ยวนี้	mai d'yō née
Later	ทีหลัง	tee lahng
A bank	ธนาคาร	ta-na-kāhn
A drugstore	ร้านขายยา	ra'ān khāi yaa
A taxi stand	ที่จอดรถเท็กซี่	tee johd roht taxi
A market	ตลาด	ta-làhd
A department store	ร้านสรรพสินค้า	rāhn sâhp-pa-sin-kà
Far; not far	ไกล ; ไม่ไกล	glai; mai glai
Left; right	ซ้าย ; ขวา	sái; kwā
Here; there	ที่นี่ ; ที่นั่น	têe-nêe; têe-náhn
Open; closed	เปิด ; ปิด	purd; pid
Beautiful	สวย	suway
How much?	เท่าไหร่?	t'ôw rai
Very expensive	แพงมาก	peng-màhk
Less expensive	ถูกลงหน่อย	thook-lóng-noy
Another color	สีอื่น	see ewn
Larger	ใหญ่กว่า	yài kwàa
Smaller	เล็กกว่า	lek kwàa

Hotel	โรงแรม	rôong-rèm
A room (with bath)	ห้อง (มีห้องน้ำ)	hông (mee hông-nám)
Today	วันนี้	wahn-nèe
Tomorrow	พรุ่งนี้	prôong-nèe
__ days*	__ วัน	__ wahn
What number?	เบอร์อะไร	burr áh-rài
Good; not good	ดี ; ไม่ดี	dee; mai-dee
A restaurant	ร้านอาหาร	rành-ah-hāhn
Soup	แกงจืด	kāng-j´rrd
Meat	เนื้อ	new-áh
Chicken	ไก่	gai
Fish	ปลา	pla'a
Eggs	ไข่	kài
Vegetables	ผัก	pahk
Rice	ข้าว	kôw
Noodles	ก๋วยเตี๋ยว	kwē-t'yōw
Drinking water	น้ำดื่ม	nāhm dim
Beer	เบียร์	beer
Coffee; tea	กาแฟ ; ชา	ka-fay; cha
Milk	นม	nôhm

*For numbers see page 299.

Dessert	ของหวาน	kong-wahn
Very delicious	อร่อยมาก	ah-ròy-máhk
Police	ตำรวจ	tâm ruòt
Doctor	หมอ	māw
Dentist	หมอฟัน	māw fun
Sick	ไม่สบาย	mai-zâ-bài
Pain	เจ็บ	jèp
Do you understand?	เข้าใจไหม	kôw jai mai
I don't understand	ไม่เข้าใจ	mâi kôw jai
Slowly	ช้า ๆ	cha'a-cha'a
Possible	เป็นไปได้	pen-pái-dài
What is this?	อันนี้อะไร	ah-nêe ah-rai

NUMBERS

0	sóon
1	nèwng
2	sawng
3	sham
4	sìi
5	hâa

6	hòk
7	jèt
8	pàet
9	kòw
10	sìp
11	sìp-ÈT
12	sìp-SAWNG
13	sìp-SAHM
14	sìp-SÌI
15	sìp-HÂA
16	sìp-HÒK
17	sìp-JÈT
18	sìp-PÀET
19	sìp-KÔW
20	YÎI-sìp
21 (etc.)	yîi-sìp-ÈT
30	SAHM-sìp
40	SÌI-sìp
50	HÂA-sìp
60	HÒK-sìp
70	JÈT-sìp
80	PÀET-sìp

90	KÔW-sìp
100	NÈWNG-roy
1000	NÈWNG-pahn
100,000	saèn
1,000,000	laán

For Telling Time

In Thailand the time can be stated in several ways. The easiest to understand is the twenty-four-hour system starting with 1 A.M.

What time is it?	Way la ah-RYE?
It is nine (A.M.)	Kôw NAA-lee-kaa
Fifteen minutes past eleven (A.M.)	Sìp-ET NAA-lee-kaa sìp-HÂA NAN-tee
Twenty minutes to ten (A.M.)	Eek YÎÌ-sèp NAN-tee ja sìp NAA-lee-kaa
Half past two (P.M.) (14 hours, 30 minutes)	Sìp-SÌI NAA-lee-kaa SAHM-sìp NAN-tee

THAI

"Thailand" in Thai is *Muang Thai,* which means "Land of the Free." The name is appropriate since

Thailand (or Siam, as it used to be called) is one of the few Asian countries never to be conquered or annexed by Western nations as they acquired colonies thoughout the world.

The language of Thailand (also used in Laos and elsewhere) is ancient. For the most part it is composed of words of one syllable, each with its own meaning, as is the case with Chinese. These separate syllables are frequently combined to make longer words. The Thai system of writing is a syllabic alphabet, adapted by King Ram Khamhang about a thousand years ago from several scripts used in southern Asia.

Thai emphasizes the gender of the person speaking. When a man says "I" he uses *pom pom,* while a woman uses *dee chan.* In addition, when finishing a sentence, whether salutation, inquiry, or statement, it is customary for a man to finish with the word *kráb,* showing that a man has spoken, while a female uses the word *ká* at the end of a sentence, to show that a woman has spoken. While not absolutely necessary, this unusual construction is generally used and considered more polite. You will certainly hear it used with great frequency by the courteous Thai people.

THAI WORDS YOU ALREADY KNOW

Some English words have been imported into Thailand. These include *bia* (beer), *Amerika, baa* (bar), *satamp* (stamp), *witaamin* (vitamin), *dollar, menu, sodaa* (soda water), and *aspirin.*

An interesting linguistic aside: The English term "white elephant" has its roots in Thailand. The phrase, which refers to an expensive property or something quite costly to maintain, derives from a Thai custom concerning these rare beasts, which occasionally could be found in the forest or among semi-domesticated herds. White elephants were considered sacred and the immediate property of the king. The ruler would take charge of the elephant and assume the high expense of caretaking befitting its sacred station. Sometimes when a nobleman grew too rich and powerful, it is reported, the king made a present of a white elephant to the proud lord. Since the king was giving it, it could not be refused, and the animal's subsequent upkeep depleted the nobleman's personal treasury so much that he ceased to be a serious threat, not being able to afford the cost of a rebellion.

SOME COMMON EXPRESSIONS

kūn po-ét PA-sa Thai dái mài	Do you speak Thai?
kūn ben kohn Ah-me-ri-kaan chái mái	Are you American?
kūn ben kohn AHN-grit chái mái	Are you English?

yin dee dóhn ràp	Welcome
chai yô	Good health
kūn tong kan a-rai?	What do you wish?
pom mái sâ'a	I don't know (m)
dee chan mái sâ'a	I don't know (f)
bāi nái kūn jal	Where are you going?
phop gan mai	See you again
ra wâng	Be careful
seu-ah	Tiger
châng	Elephant
n'goo	Snake

On a lighter note:

kūn sway mark	You are very attractive
pom chap kūn	I like you (man to woman)
dee-chan chap kūn	I like you (woman to man)
chap koon	Dear one

and otherwise:

bai hai pan	Go away!
kon gnaw	Foolish one
Far rang	Foreigner

KOREAN

Korean	한글	han´GUL

NOTE: Korean can be written horizontally, from left to right, or vertically, in columns starting on the right and moving to the left. It is often written with Chinese characters representing some of the Korean syllable combinations, although the current tendency is to avoid Chinese symbols in favor of Korean script.

Good day	안녕하십니까	ahn-N´YAHNG-ha-SHIM-nee-ka
Good evening	안녕하십니까	ahn-N´YAHNG-ha-SHIM-nee-ka
How are you?	어떻게 지내십니까	ahd-da kay chee neh SHIM-nee-ka
Very well	잘 있읍니까	jahl-ee-SUM-nee-ka
Happy to meet you	반갑습니다	bahn-gahp-SUM-nee-da
Good-bye	안녕히 가십시오	ahn-n´yahng-hee-ka-SHIP-shee-o
My name	제 이름은	jeh-ee-room-MOON
Your name	당신의 이름은	dahng-shin-uy ee-room-MOON

Mr. (and) Mrs.	씨-와-부인	shee-wa-boo-yin (after name)
Miss	양	yang (before name)
Yes	예	yeh
No; not	안이요; 않	ahn-i-yo; ahn
Excuse me	죄송합니다	jay song HAM-nee-da
Please	주십시오	joo SHIP-shee-o
Thank you	고맙습니다	goh-map-SUM-nee-da
You're welcome	천만에요	chahn-MAHN-eh-yo
Again	또	doh
Wait	기다리십시오	gee-da-ree-SHIP-shee-o
Enough	됐읍니다	dweh SUM-nee-da
Where is __	__ 어디에 있읍니까	__ oh-dee-ay ee-SUM-nee-ka
the telephone	전화	jan-hwa
the toilet	화장실	hwa jang shil
the airport	공항	kong hang
the train station	역전	yohk-chahn

the subway	지하철	jee-ha-chahl
my baggage	제 가방	jeh ka-bahng
the train for __	__ 가는 기차	__ ka-NOON kee-CHA
the bus for __	__ 가는 뻐스	__ ka-NOON BOA-su
the boat for __	__ 가는 배	__ ka-NOON beh
What time ?	몇시입니까	m´yaht shih-NEE-ka
Now; not now	지금; 지금않돼	chi-kum; chi-kum an-dweh
Later	나중에	na joong ay
A bank	은행	oon heng
A drugstore	약방	yak bahng
A taxi	택시	tek-shee
A market	시장	shee-jahng
A department store	백화점	bek-hwa-jahm
Far; not far	멀리; 가까운	muhl-lee; ka-ka-oon
Left; right	왼쪽; 오른쪽	wayn chok; o roon chok

Here; there	여기; 거기	yo-ghee; kuh-ghee
Open; closed	열림; 닫힘	yahl-lim; ta-chim
Beautiful	아름다은	ah-room-da-oon
How much?	얼마 입니까?	uhl-ma IM-nee-ka
Very expensive	너무 비싸요	nuh moo bee sa yo
Less expensive	싸요	sa yo
Another color	다른 색	dar-roon sek
Larger	더큰	duh kun
Smaller	더작은	duh cha-gun
Hotel	호텔	ho-tel
A room (with bath)	방 (목욕실)	bahng (mok yok shil)
Today	오늘	o-nul
Tomorrow	내일	neh-il
__ days*	__ 일	__ il
What number?	몇 번호	myat buhn-ho
Good; not good	좋다; 않좋다	cho-ta; an cho-ta
A restaurant	식당	shik tahng
Soup	국	gook
Meat	고기	go-ghee

*For numbers see page 311.

Chicken	닭고기	dahk go-gee
Fish	생선	seng-sun
Omelet	오믈렛	o-mu-layt
Vegetables	야채	ya-cheh
Rice	밥	bab
Bread	빵	bahng
Water	물	mool
Wine (or) beer	포도주-(이)나-맥주	po-doh-choo (ee-na) mek-joo
Coffee; tea	코오피; 차	ko-o-pee; cha
Milk	우유	oo-yoo
Dessert	디저어트	dee-ja-a-too
Delicious	맛이 좋습니다	ma-shee-cho-SUM-nee-da
Police	경찰	kyung-chahl
Doctor	의사	wee-sa
Dentist	치과의사	chee-gwa wee-sa
Pain	아픕니다	a-PUM-nee-da
Sick	병	p´yong
Do you understand?	이해 하십니까	ee-heh ha-SHIM-nee-ka
I don't understand	잘 이해 못합니다	jal ee heh mot HAM-nee-da

Slowly	천천히	chun-chun-hee
Possible	할 수 있읍니다	hal soo ee-SUM-nee-da
What is this ?	이것은 무엇입니까	ee gut see moo a-shim-nee-ka

NUMBERS

The Korean language has two sets of numbers, native Korean and Chinese-Korean. The numbers 0 through 12 are given here first in native Korean, then in Chinese-Korean. (When telling time, the hours are said in native Korean and the minutes in Chinese-Korean.) All the numbers above 12 are given in Chinese-Korean only, as this is more widely used in daily encounters.

	NATIVE KOREAN	CHINESE-KOREAN
0	yong	guan
1	ha-na	eel
2	tool	ee
3	set	sahm
4	net	sa
5	ta-soht	oh
6	yo-soht	yook
7	eel-gop	ch'eel

8	yo-dohl	p'ahl
9	ah-hoop	koo
10	yohl	sip
11	yohl-ha-na	sip-PEEL
12	yohl-tool	sip-PEE

13	sip-SAM
14	sip-SA
15	sip-O
16	sip-YOOK
17	sip-CH'EEL
18	sip-P'AHL
19	sip-KOO
20	ee-SEEP
21 (etc.)	ee-seep-EEL
30	sahm-SEEP
40	sa-SEEP
50	oh-SEEP
60	yook-SEEP
70	ch'eel-SEEP
80	p'ahl-SEEP
90	koo-SEEP

100	eel-PAYK
1,000	eel-CH'OHN
10,000	see-MAHN
1,000,000	paing-MAHN

For Telling Time

What time is it?	chee-GUM an-YOT-see IP-nee-ka
It's eight o'clock	chee-GUM yo-DOHL-see IP-nee-da
It's half past three	chee-GUM set-see-PAHN IP-nee-da
It's five to ten	chee-GUM YOHL-see o-PUN chun-IP-nee-da

KOREAN

Korean is spoken in North and South Korea by more than 70 million people and by thousands of others in Japan, the United States, and elsewhere. The written language resembles neither Chinese nor Japanese. Korean did once employ Chinese ideographs, however. In South Korea they are still used to some extent, often mixed in with Korean writing, but this is not the case in North Korea.

The invention of the special Korean syllable script is attributed to King Sejong, who ruled Korea hundreds of years ago. The king wanted to simplify writing, with a script that would give full play to the pronounciation of the language. After a number of attempts he produced one that seemed eminently satisfactory, but he imagined (rightly) the established priesthood would refuse anything new that interfered with old texts written in Chinese ideographs. King Sejong is said to have painted the new alphabet on large padamus leaves with honey; he then left them on the porch of a temple. By the next morning ants had eaten the honey, leaving clear cut-outs of the letters. The king took the leaves to the monks, who studied them until one monk said, "Perhaps these could be letters—sent by heaven to perpetuate our language!" The other monks agreed and, with King Sejong's advice, worked out the Korean syllables in the Hangul script that is used today. King Sejong, satisfied that the alphabet had been accepted, could not refrain from a certain pride of authorship. He was reported to have said: "Talented persons will learn Hangul in a single morning, and even foolish ones will understand it in ten days. There are practically no sounds that cannot be expressed by Hangul; even the sound of wind and the barking of dogs can be exactly transcribed with it."

The similarity between the words *ajashi,* "Mister" or "Sir," and *agashi,* "Miss" (the polite form of address, used without the individual's name), is a source of amusement among Koreans. Foreigners often confuse or mispronounce these words;

mixing "j" and "g" sounds can easily result in addressing a woman as "Sir" or a man as "Miss." A less amusing example of language misunderstanding and the reduction of an honorable word to slang occurred with *Meguk* and *Hanguk,* meaning, respectively, "America" and "Korea." When Koreans spoke these words, U.S. soldiers caught only the syllable *guk*—"country" or "nation"— which sounded like "gook." This word became a highly derogatory American slang term for East Asian peoples, and should be studiously avoided.

Among Korean words that should be easy to remember are a number that come from English. Here are a few: *radio, aiskrim, jeep, koktel pati, wiski, soda, hotel, taeksi, cabaret,* and *kopi* (coffee).

SOME COMMON EXPRESSIONS

yo-bo-say-YO	Hello
pan-gap-SUM-nee-da	Happy to see you
gun-bae-HAP-see-da	Your health! ("Dry cup!")
an-YON-ghee DA-n'yuh o-SIP-see-yo	Have a good trip
hang-uhn-UHL BIM-nee-da	Good luck
JEH-mee chot-SUM-nik-ka	How are things?

neh-AH-joo	Just great
jot-SUM-nee-da	
CHOO-kha	Congratulations
HAM-nee-da	

And for romance:

TAN-shin o ool	I like you a lot
CHO-a HAM-nee-da	

International Words

With the increase of foreign travel and residence by English-speakers, many English words have spread around the globe, and many more will, as world travel and extended visits continue. Below are listed only a few of these "international words." It is notable that many of them are not ultimately of English origin but come from French, Greek, and other languages—and are thus especially suitable for international communication.

airport	fax	program
alphabet	golf	radio
atom	hello	reservation
ballet	hotel	restaurant
bank	license	salad
bar	magazine	sandwich
bus	mathematics	sport
business	medicine	(movie) star
camera	menu	studio
chocolate	message	supermarket
cigarette	Miss	taxi
cinema	Mister	telephone

Coca-Cola	motorcycle	television
coffee	music	temperature
communica-tions	okay	tennis
computer	opera	theater
dance	orchestra	traveler's check
doctor	passport	violin
dollar	piano	whiskey
express	police	

When saying these words in a foreign country, it is advisable to give the vowels an international pronounciation: *a, e, i, o, u,* and *y* are rendered "ah," "eh," "ee" or "ih," "oh," "oo," and "ee," respectively. Be aware of other differences as well, depending on the country. Japanese, for example, has adopted numerous English words; they are sometimes difficult to recognize because of other syllables used with them to indicate their function and because of differences in pronunciation of specific letters (e.g., English *l* is pronounced as "r" in Japanese).

A Last Word

The most effective way to develop your ability to communicate in a foreign language is to use the words you learn as much as possible with any native speaker of that language you meet. At the end of each group of eighty words is a magic question, made immortal in language teaching by my grandfather, Maximilian Berlitz, who used it in learning fifty-six languages. It is the question "What is this?" said while pointing to something. If you learn the word from a native speaker and repeat it aloud, it will stay in your memory much longer than it otherwise would. Each time you speak the new language, you will find that your vocabulary expands, since the words you know (and are therefore *reviewing*) will explain new ones. This, after all, is the natural way you learned your own language.

We wish you pleasure and success in your travels. You will find that your attempt to communicate in a foreign language will please the people you meet in that country, especially if you remember to use "Pardon me," "Please," "Thank you," and so on. Even the police become generally more pleasant and more eager to help when addressed in their native language by an English-speaking person who at least tries to adapt to the local scene.

Whenever you speak to a foreigner, use his language first. If he speaks English, so much the better; but if he does not, you have made an important and rewarding step in international relations. *Bon voyage!*